EVERYTHING IS PERMITTED

The Making of

NAKED LUNCH

Edited by Ira Silverberg

Grafton

*An Imprint of HarperCollins*Publishers

Grafton
An Imprint of HarperCollins*Publishers*
77–85 Fulham Palace Road,
Hammersmith, London W6 8JB

A Grafton Original 1992
9 8 7 6 5 4 3 2 1

Photography credits appear on page 128

A catalogue record for this book is available from the British Library

ISBN 0 586 21714 2

Special thanks to Gabriella Martinelli, whose insight and perseverance
made this book a reality.
Thanks also go to Prudence Emery, James Grauerholz, Beth Hurstein,
Don Kennison, Laura Lindgren, David Trinidad, and Sandra Tucker
for their help and support. (I.S.)

Cover and interior design by Laura Lindgren

page 1: Peter Weller
page 2: Peter Weller and Judy Davis
page 6: Peter Weller

ONTENTS

JEREMY THOMAS PRESENTS

A DAVID CRONENBERG FILM WILLIAM BURROUGHS'S NAKED LUNCH

NAKED LUNCH

PETER WELLER

JUDY DAVIS

IAN HOLM

JULIAN SANDS

MONIQUE MERCURE

NICHOLAS CAMPBELL

MICHAEL ZELNIKER

ROBERT A. SILVERMAN

JOSEPH SCORSIANI

and

ROY SCHEIDER

Casting by Deirdre Bowen

Costume Designer Denise Cronenberg

Edited by Ronald Sanders

Music by Howard Shore

Production Designer Carol Spier

Director of Photography Peter Suschitzky

Co-producer Gabriella Martinelli

Based on the book by William S. Burroughs

Produced by Jeremy Thomas

Written and Directed by David Cronenberg

Peter Weller as William Lee.

above: William S. Burroughs and Ira Silverberg.

For the literary purist, a film based on a favorite novel never quite lives up to his or her expectations. The purist might think that the filmmaker took too many liberties with the novel's plot or narrative; the screenplay might have eliminated a character from the film—one considered essential to the story or perhaps to the writer's entire oeuvre; the director or screenwriter's reinterpretation of certain scenes to stress a visual rather than literary impact might be considered aesthetically offensive. The translation of any novel to film is fraught with such disappointments for the viewer who expects a literal interpretation.

In the case of a William S. Burroughs novel, though, the purist—probably an avid student of Burroughs's entire body of work—will look for the spirit and ideas integral to the original text rather than a mirror image. The identification of Burroughsian principles is especially important to the fan in the film version of *Naked Lunch,* a novel that has been considered virtually unfilmable (a phrase you will hear throughout this book) because of its structure and transgressive nature, as well as the potential cost of creating such a visual extravaganza.

The cultural implications of William S. Burroughs's work have filtered into the general population via nonliterary media: films, music videos, records, and fine art made by both Burroughs and his artistic disciples. The Burroughs spirit has become accessible to a group much larger than just his aficionados. The proliferation of his images, ideas, and language has become something of a phenomenon and has elevated Burroughs to the status of cultural icon.

With David Cronenberg's *Naked Lunch,* this infiltration occurs in the most direct and effective method to date. By making *Naked Lunch,* David Cronenberg expands the boundaries of what has traditionally been acceptable in film, providing the ultimate testimony to a writer whose work altered the course of postwar letters and opened the door to the postmodern society in which we now live.

Everything Is Permitted: The Making of Naked Lunch chronicles the development of this project. Beginning with introductions by Cronenberg and Burroughs on how their shared esteem of one another's work culminated in this film, it moves on to a portrait of the film, capturing *Naked Lunch*'s key scenes in still photography. The history of the production is documented with on-set anecdotes from the cast and crew accompanied by behind-the-scene shots. An explanation and visual record of the development and production of the film's special effects, created by the Academy Award–winning special-effects company CWI, illuminates the unique meeting of minds in the film. Finally, the artistic sensibilities of Burroughs and Cronenberg are examined in a more critical fashion, putting this project into perspective for the reader recently introduced to (as well as those already familiar with) the work of either artist.

More than just a book about the making of a motion picture, *Everything Is Permitted: The Making of Naked Lunch* is about the dissemination of seemingly transgressive ideas, understanding a director's approach to explaining the process of writing, and ultimately, is a testament to the power of the writer and the dangers inherent in the act of writing.

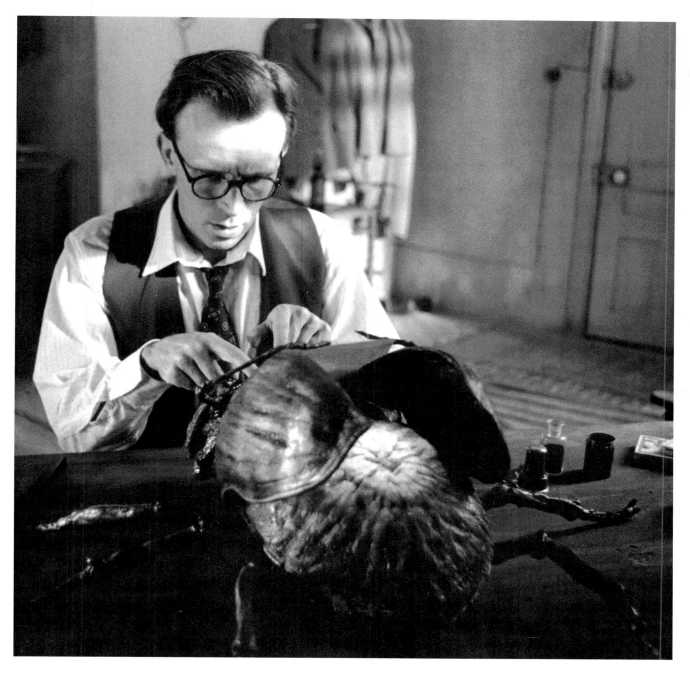

Peter Weller writing on the Bugwriter.

█NTRODUCTION

William S. Burroughs

█ was in Tangier in 1954, writing letters to my friends Allen Ginsberg and Jack Kerouac and trying to work on my third novel. My first novel, *Junky,* had been published the year before, and my second novel, *Queer,* had been put aside as unpublishable. At that time I had no idea that the novel I was writing, then called *Interzone,* would ever be published, and much less could I have imagined that it would be interpreted by an acclaimed film director some thirty-five years later. Such are the things that can happen if you live long enough. Isn't life peculiar?

"I am having serious difficulties with my novel. I tell you the novel form is completely inadequate to express what I have to say. I don't know if I can find a form. I am very gloomy as to prospects of publication" (letter to Kerouac, August 18, 1954). But *Naked Lunch* was eventually published, in Paris in 1959, then in England and the U.S. a few years later, and it is now in print in sixteen languages.

It is probably an understatement to say that the novel does not obviously lend itself to adaptation for the screen: it has dozens of characters, few of whom are developed beyond their initial appearance; the action is set in cities all over the world; it is composed of many small, fragmentary, kaleidoscopic scenes; and there is no traditional story line. It is a novel with a great deal of talk, and the rule of film is that movies *move,* with minimal talk.

But in 1970, when I was living in London, two of my closest friends, the late Brion Gysin and Antony Balch, set out to adapt it for film. Antony had made a number of short experimental films with Brion and myself, *Towers Open Fire* and *The Cut-Ups* among them. Brion wrote a screenplay for *Naked Lunch* that was long on burlesque and included a series of music-hall comedy songs that he composed. After four years of following leads that went nowhere, that project was abandoned. In 1979 Frank Zappa came to me with the concept of *Naked Lunch* as an off-Broadway musical. This struck me—and still does—as a pregnant idea, but it was not to be.

In the early 1980s it came to my attention that David Cronenberg was interested in *Naked Lunch.* Not being an especially avid filmgoer, I was unaware of his work—but as I learned about his films, I began to understand his attraction to my novel, and to appreciate his considerable accomplishments as a filmmaker. In February of 1984 we met for the first time, in New York, and I was very favorably impressed with David's ideas for the project.

I was also relieved that David did not ask me to write or co-write the screenplay, as I am sure I would have no idea how to do so. Writers are prone to think they can *write* a film script, not realizing that film scripts are not meant to be read, but acted and photographed. After fighting my way through *The Last Words of Dutch Schultz,* I had at least learned that lesson.

In January 1985 Jeremy Thomas organized a visit to Tangier with David, Jeremy's associate Hercules Bellville, my secretary James Grauerholz, and myself. I had not been back toTangier since 1972, and David

had never been there. To me, the town was hardly recognizable—the Parade Bar was closed, and with the exception of my old friend Paul Bowles, there was almost no one still there from the late 1950s. But enough of the magic of the place remained for David to form some lasting impressions.

I first read David's script around Christmas of 1989. My immediate reaction was that he had crafted a masterful thriller from the disparate elements of the novel, choosing a few and discarding many others, and drawing upon parts of my other books *Exterminator!* and *Queer.* It is axiomatic that novels and

films are two very different mediums, and especially in the case of a novel like this one, with apparently no cinematic structure. I felt, and still feel, that David's script is very true to his own Muse as a filmmaker, very consistent with the high level of artistry for which he is known, and all in all most admissible interpretation of the novel and of my quasi-autobiographical, but fictional, protagonist, "Bill Lee." I also feel that David and I are indebted to Jeremy Thomas for his courage and steadfastness in bringing this unique film to completion.

I was dismayed, naturally, to see the scenes that David wrote in which "Bill Lee" shoots his wife, "Joan"; but on reflection, I feel that the scenes in his script are so different from the tragic and painful episodes in my own life from which he drew his inspiration that no intelligent person can mistake the movie for a factual account. I reconciled myself to the idea that I must, as the saying goes, "trust the director."

For reasons best known to himself, David chose to treat "Lee's" homosexuality as a somewhat unwelcome accident of circumstance and plot, rather than as an innate characteristic. Whether this is because of David's own heterosexuality, or his assessment of the realities of making and releasing a multi-million-dollar movie, or to other factors, I cannot say. Probably he simply did not, as an artist, find that aspect of "Lee" to be significant to the story he wanted to tell in the film.

David's substitution of imaginary drugs—such as bug powder, the black meat, and Mugwump jissom—for the rather more mundane heroin and marijuana depicted in the novel is a masterstroke. One of the novel's central ideas is that addiction can be metaphorical, and what could underscore this better than the film's avoidance of actual narcotics? Clearly, what interested David about *Naked Lunch* was the idea that the protagonist finds himself conscripted as an agent or operative of forces whose identity, and purposes, are anything but clear to him. "Lee's" escalating addiction to these fictional substances is merely part of a larger scenario in which he is unwittingly and unwillingly enlisted by these unseen forces.

As this movie—developed in an atmosphere of mutual friendship and respect for the director and producers—nears release, I feel both apprehension and exhilaration. I hope it will be as good as I believe it to be, and as well received as I expect it will be. I hope that my readers will judge the film as something quite apart from my novel, and that I may perhaps find some new readers thereby.

Raymond Chandler was once asked, "How do you feel about what Hollywood has done to your novels?" He reportedly answered, "My novels? Why, Hollywood hasn't done anything to them. They're still right there, on the shelf." David Cronenberg's *Naked Lunch* is an ambitious and daring effort. I look forward to seeing it on the silver screen.

September 1991

INTRODUCTION

David Cronenberg

Was I possessed by the writing spirit of William S. Burroughs? First in the airplane taking me to London, and later in the rented house in St. John's Wood, I would find myself cackling demonically over some wickedly deadpan dialogue exchange I had just written, dialogue I knew might possibly have already been written by Burroughs without my conscious knowledge. Or that could have been written by Burroughs, or that might in the future be written by Burroughs. I spent almost three months there in the big, empty house while playing the role of a serial-killing psychotherapist in Clive Barker's film *Nightbreed,* and it was the closest thing to "automatic writing" I have ever experienced. In my delirium I thought that should Burroughs die while I was writing the script for *Naked Lunch,* I would just keep on writing beyond the script, just write Burroughs's next book for him, his next several books . . .

A conceit which, to my shame and relief, was only a conceit. For Burroughs was at that very moment writing things I could barely imagine, never mind anticipate, never mind create out of myself, and I was toiling away in some bizarre time warp of the fifties, cooking up a new/old naked lunch for the cinema. And then there were the differences: between the written word and the movies, between Burroughs and me, between gay and straight, between the fifties and the nineties, between Americans and Canadians.

Jeremy Thomas and I met at the Toronto Film Festival in 1984, to which he had brought his Stephen Frears film, *The Hit.* "They tell me you want to do a film of *Naked Lunch,*" he said.

opposite: David Cronenberg.

above: Cronenberg on location.

"Well, yes, I accidentally said that to an interviewer, once. I was surprised to hear myself saying it."

"That's a film I desperately want to produce. Do you know Burroughs? Why don't we all go to Tangier and talk about it?"

We all did go to Tangier, and walked the streets with Burroughs, and met the living remnants of his past (our somewhat biased point of view), the men who still ran the Tanger Inn, the American writer Paul Bowles, a Moroccan in the street who recognized Burroughs and almost fell over to see him. He had been nine years old when he last saw him and said Burroughs looked the same except for the cane.

I went to Burroughs's seventieth birthday party in New York City, a raucous, star-studded affair at the Limelight. I went to his more subdued seventy-fifth at his home in Lawrence, Kansas. Five years visibly, palpably gone by and I still hadn't written the script. I was probably afraid to. It was a book that was acknowledged by all, myself included, to be impossible to translate to the screen. Maybe the key word was "translate." Yes: I was too arrogant to be a mere translator. I was not born to be a translator. What was I doing with Burroughs's book, then? one might ask.

I certainly asked. I asked Burroughs a lot of questions over the years, questions that might have been thought unlikely for a translator. I asked him his thoughts about the danger inherent in dying and passing on to an afterlife. ("You could end up in the wrong company.") About his insect imagery, all of it negative, as in "Sailor's dead insect eyes." ("Well, butterflies are all right.") About the overlapping of life and art. And would it be all right if I somehow ended up betraying his sexual sensibility, since mine was in so many ways different?

I did not find myself asking him what kind of movie he thought I should make out of his book. He was, after all, not a filmmaker, but the Pope of Interzone. I wanted him to bless the endeavor, bless the vessel about to embark on the perilous voyage, bless the (possibly unholy) fusion of my art and his. I wanted to do penance before committing the sin. We went out shooting pistols in the dead of winter in Kansas, our hands red and stiff and shaky. We thought we were both pretty good shots, considering. Later we watched tapes of Burroughs's rushes, unedited footage of his role in *Drugstore Cowboy*. We thought he gave a pretty good performance, considering.

And eventually, after some years, I was quietly possessed by the spirit, not the evil, ugly spirit that can take you by surprise, but the mordantly playful, the guardedly passionate, the funny, the tragic, the cosmic writing spirit of Burroughs, and then without any trouble at all, and hardly being aware of it, I wrote the script for *Naked Lunch*. And then I had to make the movie.

August 1991

PORTRAIT OF THE FILM

The time is 1953. The place is New York, in the grip of winter. And William Lee, former junkie turned pest exterminator extraordinaire, is making his daily rounds, killing cockroaches for the citizens with his canister of poison. Until like the insects themselves, his wife, Joan, becomes hooked on the yellow poison powder and Lee's grim little life starts to whirl out of control.

Two narcotics detectives take him in for questioning and confront him with a giant talking beetle that craves poison and claims to be Lee's controller in some bizarre spy operation. Back at home, Lee finds Joan's addiction to bug powder has grown insatiable, and he visits the malevolent Dr. Benway, who prescribes an even stronger narcotic made from the flesh of giant Brazilian black centipedes. Returning home, he finds Joan on the couch making love to his best friend. When Lee and Joan play their "William Tell" routine, Lee shoots her dead and goes on the run.

Dazed and crazed, Lee runs from encounter to encounter, each more hallucinatory than the last. In a dark dockside bar he meets his first Mugwump, a powerful and sexually menacing alien from Interzone. In a pawn shop he trades his gun for a portable typewriter that later sprouts legs and wings, transforming itself into a grotesque intelligent mechanical insect that insists it is Lee's controller and that Lee is a spy. On fleeing to Interzone, Lee discovers a closed city full of blinding light and bohemian decadence, a nightmarish version of Casablanca in which drugs, boys, betrayal, and sex are the currency in a power struggle he does not understand.

Among the expatriates Lee meets in this sinister zone are Hans, a German drug baron and purveyor of the deadly black meat; Yves Cloquet, a dissipated Swiss with a

above: Peter Weller.

taste for giving pain and absorbing young flesh; and most importantly, Tom and Joan Frost, decadent American writers whose marriage conceals a dark secret.

Locked in his hotel room, writing dubious reports on his insect typewriter, Lee becomes a haunted man. In the scented nights, surrounded by Interzone boys and flying on the crest of a narcotic wave, Lee loses all sense of time, of space, and of himself. He is an agent without a superior, a spy without a country, a junkie running out of junk. But he is also writing what will become one of the most influential novels of the century, a series of reports eventually to be called *Naked Lunch*.

William Lee is an exterminator.

Inside A. J. Cohen's Exterminators.

Joan, Lee's wife, is addicted to bug powder.

The Lees at home.

"It's a Kafka high. You feel like a bug."

Hauser and O'Brien show up at A. J. Cohen's and Lee gets busted for possession of bug powder.

In the cop shop with the contraband.

Hauser leaves Lee to see if the bug powder works—
on bugs, that is. A bug gives Lee instructions for
the reports he must write.

"William Lee, I have arranged all this just to have a moment
alone with you. . . .

"I am your case officer."

The Lees do their "William Tell" routine.

In Interzone Lee meets Kiki and
Mugwump.

Kiki introduces Lee to a friend who
"specializes in sexual ambivalence."

opposite: "No point feigning surprise.
You knew we would be getting in
touch with you."

Lee meets Hans, a dealer of black centipede meat.

"You are an American, correkt?"

Lee and Hans in the drug factory.

Lee returns home to begin a report. He starts typing but soon begins to nod off after doing some black centipede powder.

The typewriter, now a bug similar to his case officer, wakes him.

Lee jolts awake and steps back toward the door. "Now, now, Bill. No need for that. You didn't think we'd abandon you, did you?"

At Café Central, Lee meets Joan and Tom Frost, American expatriate writers living in Interzone.

Later, the Frosts bring Lee to a party.

Lee never makes it home but falls asleep on Interzone beach.

opposite: Cloquet, a Swiss national, finds Lee on the beach.

Lee's typewriter demonstrates some of the dangers of writing.

opposite: Lee and Joan Frost share
an intimate moment . . .

with a sex blob . . .

and Fadela, the Frosts' housekeeper.

Later, Lee and Joan search for Fadela . . .

and find her in the market dealing the meat of the black centipede.

Tom Frost points out more of the
dangers of writing.

Lee's friends Martin and Hank find him on Interzone beach.

"We thought it was important for us to help
you get your book together."

Later, Lee sees them off.

"I think Bill's on top of things, don't you?"
"He has a grip on a certain unique reality principle, yes."

"If we fix the typing machine, will we also fix the life?"

Lee and Kiki go to the forge to repair Lee's typewriter.

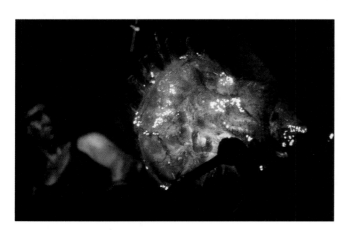

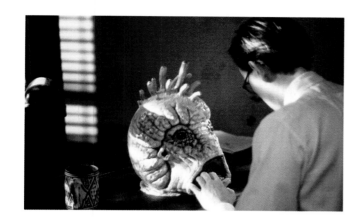

Lee works with the new Mugwriter that Kiki
helped him to get from the forge.

"I am very proud to be your friend, you know.
I am very proud that I can help you to be a writer."

Lee and Kiki take a ride with Cloquet to his house . . .

where Cloquet makes a pass at Kiki.

*Lee hears screams coming
from the bird room . . .*

where he finds Kiki and Cloquet.

Lee finds Joan in the Mugwump dispensary . . .

*where Hans, along with many other
Interzoners, has become a slave to
Mugwump jissom.*

who is, in fact, the elusive Dr. Benway.

Lee and Joan leave Interzone for Annexia, where they do their "William Tell" routine.

PRODUCTION HISTORY

*Prudence Emery
and Ira Silverberg*

In David Cronenberg's free adaptation of William S. Burroughs's surrealistic literary classic *Naked Lunch,* a writer who fears his own talent becomes liberated when mysterious forces send him on a nightmarish adventure in Interzone: a fictitious place populated by spies, junkies, witches, and mutating monsters.

Cronenberg's version of *Naked Lunch* stars Peter Weller, Judy Davis, Ian Holm, Julian Sands, Monique Mercure, Nicholas Campbell, Michael Zelniker, Joseph Scorsiani, Robert A. Silverman, and Roy Scheider. Produced by Jeremy Thomas with Gabriella Martinelli as co-producer, the United Kingdom–Canada co-production was filmed over three months on location in Toronto in early 1991, from a screenplay by David Cronenberg.

The seeds of the screenplay had been germinating ever since Cronenberg first read *Naked Lunch,* more than thirty years ago. At that time Cronenberg was an aspiring novelist whose other primary literary influence was Vladimir Nabokov. He found himself writing under the towering shadow of these two formidable authors, creating pastiches of their work.

When Cronenberg later set his sights on filmmaking, he felt free to invent his own unique cinema, not laboring under the same perception of any filmmakers. Nonetheless the literary influences, particularly that of Burroughs, remained strong within him.

"Eventually as I began to get a grip on my own cinematic voice, I started to think it would be very interesting if I returned to one of my own two main roots and tried to adapt *Naked Lunch* to the screen," recalls Cronenberg.

*above: David Cronenberg,
William S. Burroughs,
and Peter Weller.*

Producer Jeremy Thomas on the set.

That was more than a decade ago. In 1984, when producer Jeremy Thomas attended Toronto's Festival of Festivals, he tracked Cronenberg down. "I had heard that David wanted to do a film of *Naked Lunch,* and I wanted to produce it. I was fascinated with David's films and the Burroughs book. I thought that the combination of the two would be a recipe for a wonderful film," says Thomas, who subsequently optioned the book for a film.

Cronenberg met Burroughs for the first time in 1984 at the author's legendary seventieth birthday party at the Limelight Night Club in New York City. The following year Cronenberg, Burroughs, and Thomas traveled to Tangier, the city where Burroughs wrote his counterculture classic during the fifties. His works, together with those of his friends Allen Ginsberg and Jack Kerouac, launched the Beat movement. The title *Naked Lunch* was Kerouac's invention.

"We retraced the footsteps of *Naked Lunch* and got stuck in Tangier because the weather closed in and we were stranded in Interzone," says Thomas. Interzone was an International Zone in Tangier inhabited by artists seeking a tax- and harrassment-free haven. In the film, Interzone is an imaginary place based upon this actual sector.

Thomas, producer of Bernardo Bertolucci's film *The Last Emperor,* which won nine Oscars, and Cronenberg, who also won an Academy Award for *The Fly,* began the process of making *Naked Lunch* in 1985. "We figured that this was the time to get serious about making this movie, which we knew was going to be difficult," says Cronenberg.

The first attempt to make a film of *Naked Lunch* occurred in 1971, when the painter and writer Brion Gysin, a longtime friend of Burroughs, wrote a script to be directed by Antony

William Burroughs with a Bugwriter.

Balch and star Mick Jagger. But this endeavor never got off the ground. The following year television producer Chuck Barris gave it a try, with Terry Southern in mind for the screenwriter. This effort too never got anywhere. "This is the first really feasible attempt to put it on screen," commented Burroughs on a visit to the set in Toronto to watch the filming.

Although he was impressed with Cronenberg's films *The Fly* and *Dead Ringers,* Burroughs had never seen *Scanners.* However, as the famous exploding head scene and the focus on telepathic forces in *Scanners* achieved cult status, Burroughs found that Cronenberg's vision struck a responsive chord in him. Cronenberg's themes reflected those which had always preoccupied Burroughs. "When I heard that David was interested in doing the film," says Burroughs, "I thought . . . he's the one that can do it if anyone can." Furthermore, Burroughs didn't

want to take on the task of writing the script himself, and he knew Cronenberg to be an interesting writer in his own right.

While both Cronenberg and Thomas had achieved financial and critical success, financing *Naked Lunch* was something of a challenge. "Raising the funds for the film proved to be a daunting experience because I foolishly put in my sales brochure 'the unfilmable *Naked Lunch,*' " says Thomas.

"It's impossible to make a movie out of *Naked Lunch.* A literal translation just wouldn't work. It would cost $400 million to make and would be banned in every country in the world—not an attractive proposition for a producer," says Cronenberg. "It was obvious, for both artistic and practical reasons, I was going to have to do my own version of *Naked Lunch*—a fusion of my own writing with Burroughs's."

"It's very difficult to translate any book exactly to the

Cronenberg and Burroughs on the set.

Slaves to the jissom (Cronenberg's invented drug).

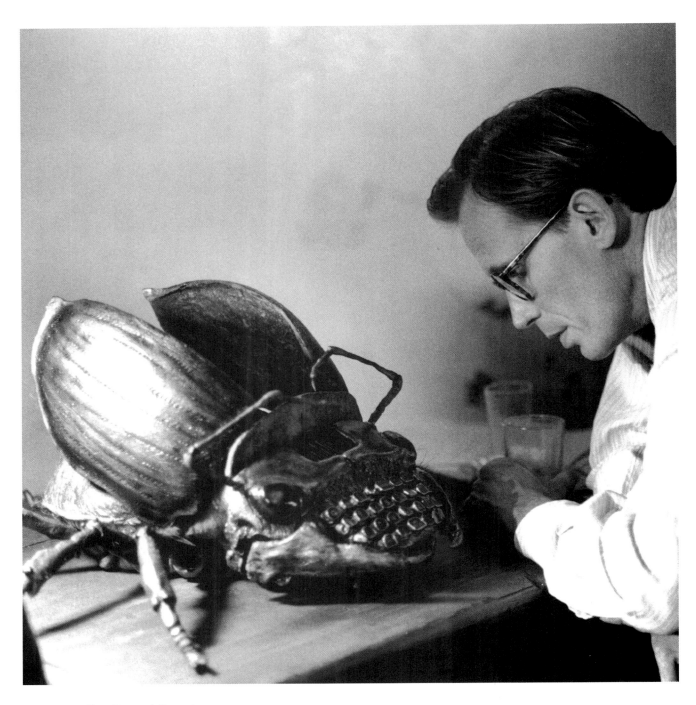

Weller as William Lee with Bugwriter.

screen, especially a book like this. It's really more the spirit of the book in the film," explains Thomas.

Throughout the years of development on Cronenberg and Thomas's *Naked Lunch,* Burroughs remained enthusiastic and supportive. "He helped us every way possible to make it happen," says Cronenberg. The director talked with Burroughs off and on during the five years of the film's development. He visited his home in Lawrence, Kansas, to discuss the project in detail. "I didn't want to mislead him or [make him] think that the movie was going to end up being something that it wasn't," says Cronenberg.

The director explained to his longtime mentor that the movie would be about the act of writing *Naked Lunch,* about the commitment and danger of being creative and how that affects the person writing it. "I moved back from the page itself to include the process of writing the book," says Cronenberg, who waited until he received Burroughs's approval before going ahead. Cronenberg recalls, "I could then just let it flow, and to my surprise, when I sat down to write it, it was there. The primal act of creation is the writing of the script."

Cronenberg completed the first draft of his screenplay in 1989, while on location in England, where he was acting in Clive Barker's *Nightbreed.* "It was a good time to start writing a screenplay," he says, "because I was basically alone for a couple of months. Burroughs's book is very fragmented and dreamlike, a series of set pieces. You could read it back to front. I have given the movie a more traditional narrative structure, a psychological and emotional development, and tell the story through a main character."

Cronenberg reinterpreted Burroughs's satirical sketches

Director of photography Peter Suschitzky with Cronenberg.

Weller gets into his role.

Judy Davis as Joan Frost.

Roy Scheider as Burroughs's infamous Dr. Benway.

about drugs and homosexuality in order to be as faithful as possible to the spirit of the book. "A lot of what in Burroughs is very direct had to be done in a metaphorical way in the movie," he explains. "The theme of addiction is common to both the book and the film—addiction to things that are not drugs, particularly power and control of other people. The imagery of drugs is really meant to lead to some understanding of the phenomenon of addiction." The drugs in the film are not real; they are Cronenberg's fabrications. "Inventing my own drugs has allowed me more freedom to shape the meaning of the movie," Cronenberg adds.

Burroughs and Cronenberg have long shared a fascination with science fiction and insect imagery; it has penetrated their respective works. The Mugwumps, a pure Burroughs invention in *Naked Lunch,* were transferred to the screen as six-foot-tall reptilian creatures. Cronenberg created additional creatures: aggressive insect typewriters that talk back to their users, and the sex blob, as it was affectionately referred to on set. His inventions solved the problem of "delivering to the screen things that can't be shown in a mainstream movie."

On visiting the set, Burroughs encountered Bugwriters, Mugwriters, and Cronenberg's ideas on writing. "The film raises a very interesting question about the relationship between writers and the actual instrument," Burroughs observes.

"That's one of the things in the script that is not directly from the book," responds Cronenberg. "The book doesn't deal directly with some of the other things that the movie does—a sense of loss, the sense of opportunities lost, of people lost and trying to find their way out. As the film is about writing, I wanted to get into that element more deeply than it's been done

Monique Mercure as Fadela
whips a sex blob.

before. That meant getting a bit strange. One of the ways I've done it is to create six characters in the film who are writers. Each of them has a different understanding of what the process is, what it means, and why they do it."

Cronenberg continues, "The main character of William Lee is learning about what it is to be a writer from all these other writers, and he's doing it almost unconsciously. If he's aware of himself as a writer, he'll freeze. Somehow he manages to hallucinate himself a world in which he's been involved in an arcane spy plot; he's been suborned to be an agent and is actually writing reports for his masters, whose political position he's not really very certain of. By the end of the movie he's still denying that he's written the novel *Naked Lunch.*"

Although the film also draws on other Burroughs source material such as *Exterminator!, Queer,* and *Letters to Allen*

Ginsberg, Cronenberg explains, "The film has to be something that still deserves to be called *Naked Lunch,* accurately reflecting some of the tone of Burroughs, what his life stands for, and what his work has been—a combination of Burroughsian material but put into a structure that's not very Burroughsian. That was basically my approach." When Burroughs read the script around Christmastime 1989, he telephoned Cronenberg to say he thought it was terrific.

In June 1990, after the screenplay was finished, Cronenberg traveled to Tangier to location scout with producer Jeremy Thomas, co-producer Gabriella Martinelli, production designer Carol Spier, and director of photography Peter Suschitzky.

While Cronenberg was still writing and not yet at the casting stage, he received a letter from Peter Weller, who had heard about the project during the shoot of *RoboCop 2.* A fan of both Burroughs's books and Cronenberg's movies, he was keen to be involved with the film. He had read *Naked Lunch* in 1968, during what he calls his counterculture years. Weller found it to be "an incredible work [that] broke the form of the American novel."

Weller wrote to Cronenberg to inquire about any involvement with the project. Nine months later the two met in New York and Weller landed the lead role. In preparation to play the part of Lee, Weller met several times with Burroughs in the fall of 1990. "We talked about art, drugs, and life," recalls Weller.

Weller rereads *Naked Lunch* every few years, and on the set he was accompanied by a dog-eared copy. "There's a taste, a spirit, and an imagery from *Naked Lunch* that is a great preparation daily for me," Weller says. "Lee is trying to exorcize the great tragedy of his life by writing. But there is no way out and he's doomed to relive the experience again and again. It's a phantasmagoria of how and why he becomes a writer."

The film presented unique casting challenges for Cronenberg. "The characters are quite strange and bizarre in what they do and how they think. They have to be believable as writers and as the various things that they are in this movie—homosexuals, drug addicts, and dislocated expatriates with strange accents, all denizens of Interzone, which is literally a state of mind," says Cronenberg, whose preferred method is to cast the lead character first, and then build the cast around that actor.

"Peter Weller's presence on screen is really Burroughsian," says the director. "He has that gaunt, strange, piercing, haunting look. The audience is going to be surprised at the depth and detailing of his performance, which is absolutely sen-

Carol Spier's rendering of Interzone market.

Interzone market as Interzone beach.

sational and very profound. He has a wonderful understanding of the Burroughsian universe."

Casting Judy Davis was another story altogether. "I had quite a violent reaction to it," confides Davis, who was so horrified when she read the script, she threw it against a wall. It took eight reads and a phone call from Cronenberg to persuade her to take the two roles of Joan Lee and Joan Frost.

"I was frightened by his script, and that can be quite compelling. I felt there was something I could learn as an actress through doing it, through facing my fears. Some of the scenes I was in were so off the wall, it was liberating for me. Cronenberg himself was a bit of a lure as well, says Davis, an Australian actress who had never heard of William Burroughs before. "The novel is part of [an] American literary history that I'd never been involved in."

Davis read much material to research her role, but she steered away from reading Burroughs's novel. "The second character I play, the expatriate writer Joan Frost, was the most challenging for me," Davis recalls. "I read a great deal about expatriate American writers." Davis also perfected an American accent for her roles.

Cronenberg points out, "There are only two female characters in the film, and Judy's is the primary role. It was very important that she be able to hold her own against the homosexual maleness of the movie. I needed an actress who was very strong, powerful, magnetic, and charismatic, which she is. I think she's one of the four or five best film actresses in the world."

Having sold over a million copies throughout the world, *Naked Lunch* is a book that clearly held great appeal to actors as a film project. The distinguished British actor Ian Holm, a longtime admirer of Cronenberg's work, joined the cast. "The challenge for me was that the role of Tom Frost is about as far removed from my own personality as it is possible to imagine." Meanwhile, two more actors approached Cronenberg to express their interest: Julian Sands and Roy Scheider. "Julian has the feeling of a fallen angel. He was the right actor for the part of Yves Cloquet, a wealthy Swiss Anglophile," Cronenberg comments.

Scheider had heard about the movie from Weller and wanted to play the perverted, quintessentially American Dr. Benway. "The book is about as bizarre, as perverse, and as erotically aberrant as anything I can think of. Burroughs, who was thirty years ahead of his time, is capable of wild, flowing, vivid prose that is gorgeous in its horrendous description," says Scheider, who was avidly curious about how Cronenberg would handle it. After reading the script, he said, "It's great. The movie

is a white paper against drug abuse. It's one big hallucinogenic nightmare and manages to offend almost everybody."

"I was just delighted an actor of his stature wanted to do it," remarks Cronenberg. He was equally delighted that the enormously talented Canadian actress Monique Mercure was interested in playing the weird Interzone witch who has a hold over some of the main characters. Michael Zelniker and Nicholas Campbell signed up to play two writers who regard Lee as their mentor, and Robert A. Silverman, who appeared in Cronenberg's films *The Brood* and *Scanners,* joined the cast to play Hans, an Interzone drug dealer. Finally, after searching in London, Madrid, and Paris, the filmmakers discovered newcomer Joseph Scorsiani in their native Toronto. Scorsiani plays Kiki, a young Interzone boy who befriends William Lee.

Upon completion of the casting, producer Jeremy

Carol Spier's rendering of the Frost apartment.

Interior of Frost apartment.

*Carol Spier's rendering
of Lee's Tangier apartment.*

Thomas remarked, "I'm thrilled with the cast, because in every film you do, when you finally decide on the actors, you discover that they are the only people who can do the roles. It's as if some unseen force brings the right people to inhabit the parts." Cronenberg agrees: "If the karma of the picture is working right, you get the people you should have in it."

One week before the commencement of principal photography, the Persian Gulf Crisis erupted. The allied invasion began on a Thursday, and filming was scheduled to begin the following Monday. The three-week shoot in Tangier was canceled. Cronenberg rewrote the script over the weekend. The film would now have to be shot completely in Toronto.

"Initially we were seduced by the fact that Burroughs wrote most of *Naked Lunch* in Tangier. The war forced me to come to terms with the fact that Interzone is really an hallucinatory state of mind," says Cronenberg. "The film became more internalized and hallucinatory, so that one understands by the end of the film that Lee never really leaves New York City. He has hallucinated a quasi-exotic kind of North Africa where he's gone to escape to write his book. It clarified the script and brought out a lot of interconnections that were hidden before."

The last-minute switch from Tangier to Toronto forced production designer Carol Spier to scramble. She changed her design concept from 1953 realism to one of realistic illusion. "The environment around Bill Lee is all in his mind," explains Spier. To depict this transitory state, Spier selected elements from Lee's experiences and placed them with bits of New York into exotic Interzone settings, such as a New York fire hydrant in a casbah courtyard. "David likes bizarre things to happen in natural settings so it looks like it could happen to anybody," said Spier, whose mammoth task was to design and construct at least seven major sets to replace the Tangier locations after filming had already started.

Among Spier's remarkable settings are:

The casbah: A maze of streets built in studio on different levels, featuring sidewalk cafés, exotic shops, a Mugwump forge, and a central courtyard large enough to accommodate 150 extras and a couple of donkeys. Spier's meticulousness is evident in such details as the presence of moss between terra-cotta roof tiles and a bird's nest atop a plinth. A New York bar and alley can be glimpsed through Moorish arches.

The black meat concession: A large factory where the black centipede meat is processed into an addictive drug coveted by William Lee.

The bus depot: The replacement for Tangier Harbor in a farewell scene. Finding 1950s buses in the 1990s proved a challenge. The film's transportation department spotted in a frozen field a vintage bus mired in mud up to its axle. Using picks and a bulldozer, six men managed to haul it out. A fresh coat of paint was slapped on, Arabic added, and it was picture-perfect.

The Tangier market: The nostrils of 200 extras were assailed by the odor of spices, fruits, flowers, and vegetables, which vied with fresh fish and meat whisked into refrigerated trucks in between takes. Moroccan artifacts, djellabas, and donkeys were juxtaposed against a strange stall where a turbaned woman sliced black centipede meat steaks, surrounded by dangling giant centipedes.

The New York market: After removal of all the Arab signage and exotica, with the exception of small dried centipedes—one of the various images that recur throughout the film—the New York market was converted from the Tangier market.

Interzone beach: Seven hundred tons of sand were brought to cover a nine-thousand-square-foot area where Bedouins gesticulated around glowing fires outside tents and where William Lee slumped against a dilapidated overturned boat. Two camels born in captivity, Clementine and Jonathan, trod on their first desert here.

The Mugwump dispensary: An enormous barn housing fifty Mugwumps suspended horizontally and attended to by a hundred "slaves." Of the hundred extras, all of whom were forewarned of this scene's weird nature, three defected. One of the defectors, a lawyer, said, "I just can't have my clients see me sucking on a Mugwump teat," and fled.

One visitor who thoroughly enjoyed his encounter with a Mugwump, however, was Burroughs. "I was impressed with the Mugwump," he says. "He's very engaging, rather simpatico." Peter Weller agrees: "In the book and in the screenplay, there's an endowed humanity in the Mugwumps." This rather worried Cronenberg, who had designed the Mugwumps—who smoke, drink, and talk—to resemble old, elongated junkies that represent

Interior of Lee's Tangier apartment.

Special-effects supervisor Jim Isaac explaining
Mugwump movements to Burroughs.

the evil spirit pervading the film.

During the set tour, Burroughs, Cronenberg, and Weller wore fedoras, reminiscent of the 1950s pulp novel hard-boiled detectives portrayed in both the book and the film. "All the clothes relate to the year 1953," explains costume designer Denise Cronenberg. The Interzone Arab extras—all of whom were immigrants to Canada from various Middle Eastern countries—wore authentic 1950s imported djellabas. The intermingling tourists also sported vintage outfits from the period.

If Denise Cronenberg couldn't find it, she made it. She had twenty-two suits tailored for Peter Weller from authentic 1950s fabric that she purchased at a New York specialty store. "You can't get that brown color any more," she notes.

Naked Lunch reunited Cronenberg with the special-effects house CWI (Chris Walas, Inc.), headed by Chris Walas, who

along with Stephan Dupuis won an Oscar for special makeup effects in *The Fly.* Nine months before principal photography began, Cronenberg discussed his ideas with Walas and Dupuis. Within three months the team, along with special-effects supervisor Jim Isaac, submitted their designs to the director.

Back in San Rafael, California, the home of CWI, the creatures were sculpted and reproduced, loaded onto a truck, and shipped up to Toronto. Customs officials at the United States–Canada border were no doubt amused when they read the list of items to declare: fifty Mugwumps, four typewriter creatures, several leaping sex blobs, and forty black centipedes of varying lengths, plus forty different mechanical rigs.

"The big challenge in this show is that these creatures are real characters. We have to believe one hundred percent that they are alive, and even come to care for them," says Jim Isaac.

Roy Scheider in Fadela effects
with Cronenberg.

Cronenberg, Thomas, and Weller.

"They have one-on-one dialogue with Lee, and some required fifteen puppeteers to operate." "There's a lot of rubber that talks in this movie!" adds Cronenberg, who directed the puppets the same as actors, while someone stood alongside simultaneously speaking the dialogue. "The effects are fairly atypical in that they're somewhat raunchy and very articulate. For example, we created a flesh creature that embodies the strange sexuality of the characters in the movie," Cronenberg explains.

Director of photography Peter Suschitzky found *Naked Lunch* very demanding: "We had to work more out of order than on any film I've worked on before because of schedule changes, actors' availability, and special effects. Often we started a sequence in the middle, shot the beginning three weeks later, and left it a further three weeks before we shot the end. It was very tricky."

When Suschitzky first read the *Naked Lunch* screenplay, he felt it should look expressionistic, reminiscent of Kafka or *Dr. Caligari*. "I suggested that we do the sets like *Dr. Caligari,* but David said 'there's enough craziness in the film as it is. It should look normal. The craziness is interior.'" Suschitzky suffused the film with shadows. "It's a dark subject and takes place mostly at night. Even in the day I've put on lots of darkness and shadows." At the same time he made it quite romantic. "I've given it an overall sense of romanticism, in the artistic sense—a richness and a slight sickness that you find in Late Romanticism in German literature and art between 1900 and 1930." Peter Weller reminded him of a character in a painting by the late expressionist Otto Dix.

On working with the director, Weller says, "David Cronenberg is truly gifted in the sense that he's a man with a clear vision of what he passionately feels. He's a combination of a lucid communicator artistically and a great pragmatist. He's also a great human being—about the best you can get!"

"David is probably the most relaxed and confident director I've worked with," echoes Judy Davis. "He's very charismatic himself and unusually gentle for a director. He has a specific mind, and yet he allows actors freedom. The film should end up being both wildly comic and black, and very disturbing. That combination can make a potent experience for cinemagoers."

"Jeremy Thomas and David Cronenberg are the catalysts of *Naked Lunch*. I was thrilled to join them on such a bizarre and controversial project," says co-producer Gabriella Martinelli. "We all feel the film is in a class of its own. In it Cronenberg turns commonplace reality inside out—the effect on the viewer is much like a spontaneous hallucination. Whether it's a good or bad trip will depend on the individual. What is certain, no one will leave indifferent."

"Reading Burroughs crystallized a lot of things for me and led me into my own fantasies," rejoins Cronenberg. "It's hard to gauge the shock effect—I hope it's a kind of Burroughsian-Cronenbergesque effect."

Producer Jeremy Thomas sums it up best, saying, "I'm very satisfied that the dream David Cronenberg and I had for many years has become a reality and a most unusual film involving special effects and fantasy, and that the talents of Cronenberg and Burroughs could be harnessed together for an audience to see."

*Prudence Emery is a film publicist, and
Ira Silverberg works in book publishing.*

Naked Lunch *cast and crew.*

Judy Davis and Peter Weller.

PETER WELLER plays William Lee, a man who accidentally kills his wife and seeks to purge himself. Ultimately he discovers "that frozen moment when everyone sees what is on the end of every fork." [William S. Burroughs]

"Naked Lunch *is about a man searching for redemption for an act that is perhaps irredeemable. Bill Lee is trying to exorcise the great tragedy of his life," says Weller. "The film, which captures the spirit of Burroughs's book, follows one man's personal journey into addiction and is a fantasy of how and why he became a writer."*

JUDY DAVIS plays both Joan Lee and Joan Frost. Both are
married to writers, and both die by the hand of the same man.
*"Joan Lee is drugged out on bug powder. She's crossed
the line and there's no salvation for her. Joan Frost is a little
more together but is struggling to survive. She doesn't make it
either,"* notes Davis.

IAN HOLM portrays an American writer, Tom Frost, who lives in
Interzone with his wife, Joan, who also writes.

"Although they have an interdependent relationship, his
sexual preference is toward members of his own sex," says Holm.

JULIAN SANDS portrays Yves Cloquet, the dissolute
Swiss Anglophile.

*"Cloquet is an expatriate living in Tangier. He's an elegant
boulevardier, lascivious in his spare time, which is what I like
about him particularly. He's slightly suspect and swings every way
there is. He will have sex with anything dead or alive in any
circumstance." Sands continues, with a smile, "And he wears a
lot of jewelry on his fingers."*

MONIQUE MERCURE plays Fadela, an Interzone housekeeper-cum-witch who exerts control over the writers Tom and Joan Frost. She is also owner of the black meat drug concession.

"It's amusing that Fadela is called a housekeeper when at the same time she owns the biggest drug factory in Interzone and has all these slaves working for her," notes Mercure. *"If Cronenberg's movies are about mutation, Fadela is a creature of his fantasies—the perfect mutation. It was incredible for me to discover that Fadela is a man."*

NICHOLAS CAMPBELL plays Hank, a writer and close friend of
William Lee who, along with Martin, helps to
assemble Lee's random writings that ultimately become the
book *Naked Lunch.*

"The two characters of Hank and Martin are representa-
tives of the New York Beat generation. We're really images
and distortions in Bill's mind. It's not a straightforward
biographical treatment," says Campbell. "Trying to put the
process of writing on the screen is like mental racquet ball!"

MICHAEL ZELNIKER plays Martin, a poet and friend of Lee who travels to Interzone to help Bill with his book.

"Martin's determination to uncover the tools that will unleash and help him realize his own literary aspirations puts him in sympathy with Bill Lee and his journey," says Zelniker, who took the role because *"working on good material with the best people is what it's all about."*

Newcomer JOSEPH SCORSIANI plays Kiki, an attractive Interzone
boy who becomes involved with Bill Lee.
*"Kiki is a well-defined and yet ambiguous character," says
Scorsiani. "Although he hustles for a living, at the same time he is
innocent and naïve. He doesn't ask much from anyone and gives
much more than he's asked for."*

ROBERT A. SILVERMAN plays Hans, an Interzone drug dealer
specializing in the meat of the black centipede.

　　"Hans is a bon vivant and procurer who loves gossip,"
says Silverman. "He knows everything that's going on in
Interzone—who's doing what to whom and why! But basically
he's an agent who dabbles in drugs on the side."

Roy Scheider plays Dr. Benway, the archetypal perverted American doctor who, in prescribing an antidote drug for William Lee, only increases his addiction to the meat of the black centipede and Mugwump jissom.

Says Scheider, "Dr. Benway is probably the sleaziest scumbag in this movie. He's a manipulator, a drug user, a drug seller, an autocrat, and a dreadful person."

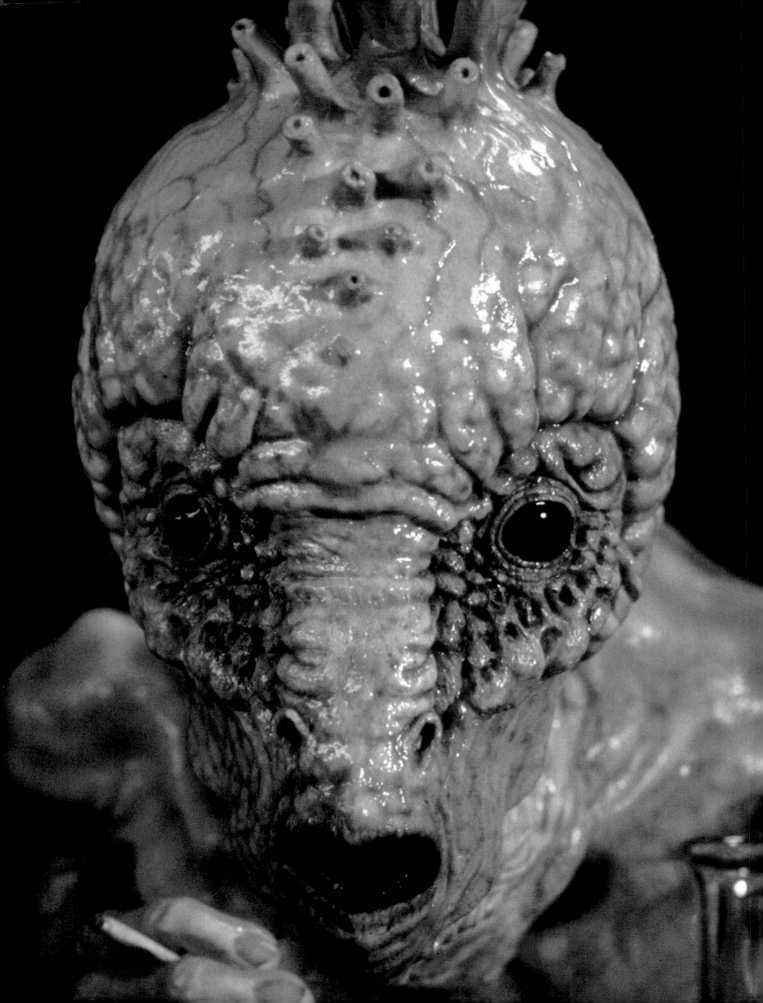

BORROWED FLESH: SPECIAL EFFECTS IN NAKED LUNCH

Jody Duncan

Even for CWI, a makeup and crea- ture-effects team accustomed to working in the realm of the fantastic, the effects called for in *Naked Lunch* were extraordinary—and extraordinarily bizarre. Founded by effects veteran Chris Walas, CWI earned a solid reputation working on such projects as Cronenberg's remake of *The Fly, Gremlins, Enemy Mine,* and *Arachnophobia,* among others. Intrigued by the unusual creatures in the script of *Naked Lunch,* and eager to collaborate with Cronenberg once again, the effects company immediately accepted the project when Cronenberg solicited its involvement in late summer of 1990. "We were very excited by the script," recalls Jim Isaac, a longtime CWI associate and effects supervisor for *Naked Lunch.* "Most of the effects in the movie were things that had never been seen before. We took the project because it was so unique, and also because we love work- ing with David. We had had a great time on *The Fly* and we really respect him as a director." Nine months before principal photography began in Toronto, Cronenberg met with key members of the Marin County–based effects facility to clarify his vision of the various creatures populating the *Naked Lunch* script. With Cronenberg's directives in mind, Stephan Dupuis—who with Walas had won an Oscar for his work on *The Fly*—began designing the creatures, creating drawings and, ultimately, foot-tall clay maquettes for the director's approval.

Among the most important of the creatures described in the script is the Mugwump—a sinister-looking yet strangely benign Interzone agent that emits through a protruding organ a powerfully addicting substance. Although many of the *Naked Lunch* creatures are products of Cronenberg's fertile imagination, the Mugwump was

opposite: a Mugwump.

above: co-producer Gabriella Martinelli, foreground, in the prop room.

Early sketches of Mugwumps.

invented by Burroughs in his novel. "Burroughs talks about the Mugwump in the book as a demure beast," says Cronenberg. "I think that it represents all of the seductive monsters we run into that have some kind of addictive element—whether it is money or power or sex or whatever."

Relying on descriptions in the book and his own instincts, Cronenberg envisioned the Mugwump as a tall, lanky creature with facial features being a cross between a wolf and Burroughs himself. "I thought his body should be like that of an old junkie—emaciated and with the 'look of borrowed flesh' that

Burroughs describes in the book. I also wanted the Mugwump to be basically humanoid, but with characteristics that would emphasize its nonhumanness." The effects team worked from Dupuis's concept drawings and old photographs of Burroughs, ultimately designing a Mugwump that features the author's jaw and elongated limbs; blue eyes, a rounded tongue, and a black beak inside its mouth. "We gave it a lizardlike coloring," Isaac comments, "with a lot of veining underneath. It also had a very pasty-looking skin—David likes that unhealthy look in his characters."

Further evolution of the Mugwump design.

opposite: Mugwump at CWI before finishing touches.

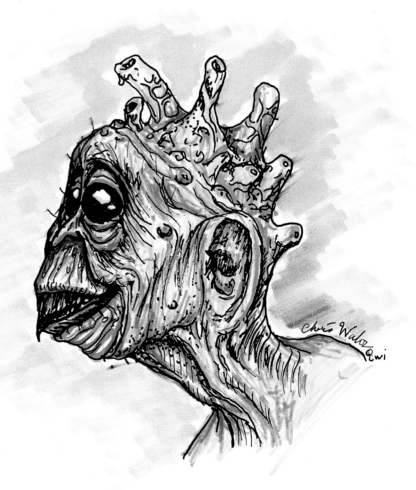

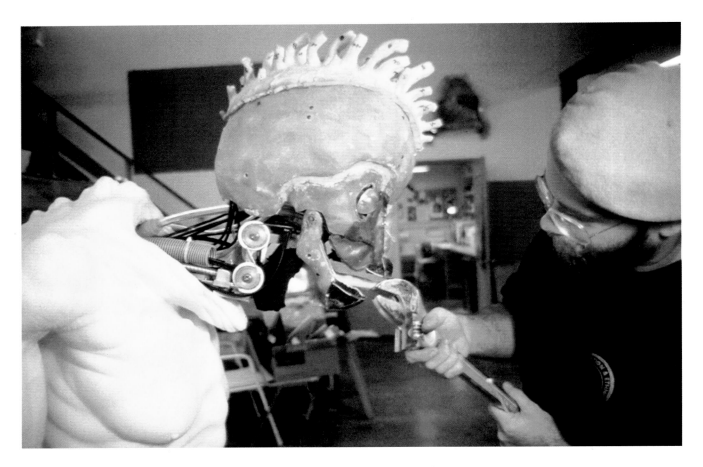

Making a Mugwump at CWI.

Because of its sexual suggestiveness, the protrusion that was to grow from the Mugwump and dispense a thick, milky substance was of particularly sensitive concern during the design phase. In the book as well as the first drafts of the script, the "teat" protrudes from the Mugwump's stomach, and characters kneel in front of the beast to suck from the organ. In an effort to desexualize the image somewhat, Cronenberg eventually opted to place the protrusions in a crest on top of the creature's head. "The idea of the teat on the head made sense," Isaac asserts, "because the Mugwump could then bend down—like a king extending his ringed hand to be kissed—and as the characters sucked it was as if they were worshiping this creature. We realized that having just one teat on the head might look silly, so we came up with the idea of the crest with several moving sea anemone–type things on top. Then only one among the moving organs would grow—which we thought would be less distracting."

Though many of the *Naked Lunch* creatures required weeks of trial and error to pin down, CWI's design for the Mugwump met with Cronenberg's immediate and enthusiastic approval. From the beginning the director had dismissed the notion that the abnormally proportioned Mugwump could be created by an actor in a suit, so upon design approval, CWI began work on a sophisticated mechanical puppet. One fully mechanical "hero" Mugwump, to be used for the creature's major dialogue scenes, was constructed. Latex-foam skins were produced in molds made from a highly detailed sculpture of the Mugwump. These skins were supported by a fiberglass understructure, into which the mechanisms to simulate various head and facial articulations were mounted.

The six-and-a-half-foot-tall hero Mugwump puppet features cable-controlled eye, mouth, and tongue movements. Air bladders inserted around the eyes and in the cheek areas provide even greater animated facial expression. Equipped with a series of pulleys and joints, the neck is capable of twisting and tilting the head from side to side. "One of the most difficult things about the Mugwump was that it had such a long neck," Isaac notes. "David really liked how that looked, but from a mechanical standpoint, it was a nightmare. The head was a good two feet from the shoulders, so we had to use very long cables to operate it—they came down through the body and then underneath the set to the puppeteers. We had cables that were up to fifteen feet long in some scenes, and generally, the longer the cable, the more difficult it is to operate the puppet."

The moving organs in the crest on top of the Mugwump's head are also mechanical, driven with cam controllers powered by a motor fitted inside the body of the puppet. In addition to the smaller moving organs, the Mugwump puppet was equipped with a latex teat capable of extending and emitting fluid. "We used air pressure to make the teat grow," explains Isaac. "Also, through the middle of the teat was a tube through which we could pump the fluid. If it was a shot where a character had to actually drink the fluid, we made up a mixture of milk and honey and egg white; for shots of it just dripping out of the teat, we used colored Methocel and egg white." Up to fifteen puppeteers were required to operate the various functions of the finished mechanical creature.

The Mugwump first appears to William Lee in a bar. Shot on a set that was raised to accommodate the puppeteers below, the puppet was mounted on the barstool with a pole extending

Cronenberg, Mugwump, and Weller on set.

Refining the Mugwumps before they're shipped to the set.　　　　　　　　*opposite: final Mugwump design.*

down through the center of its body. A T-shaped handle at the end of the pole enabled puppeteers to pivot the puppet's body at the waist or shoulders. For subsequent scenes at the forge and in Lee's apartment, the support pole was adjusted to suit the specific camera angle and setup of each particular shot.

Two articulated closeup arms were constructed for use in the bar scene, during which the Mugwump smokes and drinks. "The closeup arms were shot from the waist up," says Isaac. "The unarticulated arms that were actually attached to the puppet just hung down at its sides. For specific shots, we would bring in the closeup arms, making sure they were at the correct angle to the Mugwump's body. They had articulated fingers and wrist movement, all cable controlled. Two people were required to operate each arm."

To simulate the effect of the Mugwump smoking, a fake

cigarette—equipped with a rheostatic light at the tip—was attached to the fingers of one of the closeup arms. Air tubes inserted into the mouth and nose of the puppet allowed smoke to be exhaled. To create the smoke, the effects team first tried burning raspberry leaves in a five-gallon drum and pumping the smoke through a tube extending from the drum to the puppet. Ultimately, however, it proved more expedient—though less healthful—for a crew member to smoke a cigarette and exhale directly into the tube terminating at the puppet's nose and mouth. Bladders operated with a foot pump expanded and contracted the cheeks and chest of the puppet, adding to the realism of the smoking effect.

Less mechanically sophisticated than the hero Mugwump, a "bend-over" version was constructed for specific shots in which the creature offers the teat on its head to addicts eager to

Early drawing of Mugwriter.

Evolution of Mugwriter.

opposite: Mugwriter
model at CWI.

partake of its irresistible substance. Additionally, fifty unarticulated dummies were built for the scene in which William Lee and Kiki discover the Mugwump dispensary, a barnlike warehouse in which dozens of Mugwumps are trussed and hung upside-down, making their fluid-emitting organs easily accessible. "Some of the dummy Mugwumps had working teats," says Isaac, "and some were armatured so that we could pose them for closeup shots. To produce that kind of volume we had five Mugwump molds going at once—getting out fifty of these things was a big ordeal. Then we divided the fifty up into As, Bs, and Cs, depending on the quality of the skins. The best ones were placed nearest the camera, and the less-desirable ones were put in the back."

A variation on the Mugwump design was used for the Mugwriter, the subversive talking typewriter William Lee receives in the forge scene. Essentially a combination of a Mugwump head and a typewriter, the Mugwriter was designed with a very large mouth to accommodate Lee's hands as he reaches inside to type. However, tests conducted on the lip-synching capability of the wide-mouthed creature—which had literally pages of dialogue in the script—convinced the special-effects team to design a smaller mouth for use in the talking scenes. "The wide mouth just looked too silly when it talked," Isaac comments. "And we figured, since it was a hallucination anyway, the Mugwriter could transform itself in the course of

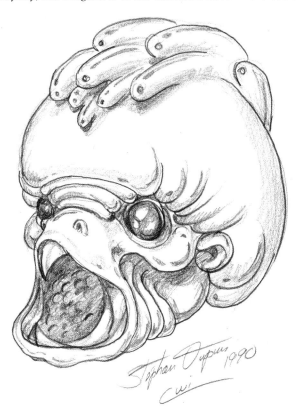

Making the Mugwriter at CWI.

the scene. So David and I brainstormed and came up with the idea of reducing the size of the mouth when it talked and then ultimately replacing it with a full Mugwump in the scene. That way we were able to have the Mugwump, rather than the Mugwriter, deliver ninety percent of the lines."

The Mugwriter was fitted with hand-cranked, rather than motorized, cam controllers to operate the movement of the teats on top of the head. "We didn't need motors on the Mugwriter because, since it was only a head as opposed to an entire body, we could easily bring cables out through the bottom and they only had to be about four feet long. The Mugwriter had the same four-way eye movement as the Mugwump. On the wide-mouthed version the lips moved independently and the mouth opened and closed. For the talking scenes we would just remove the wide mouth and replace it with the small mouth by cutting

into the jaw area and then gluing the face back on like a prosthetic." Six operators were required to articulate the mechanized Mugwriter.

In addition to the Mugwriter, a variety of "insect typewriters" is featured in the film—talking creatures that guide and at times bully William Lee as he labors to complete his "reports" from Interzone. "The insect typewriters were my trick to get the audience inside the writing experience," says Cronenberg. "Burroughs uses insect imagery a lot, and I've always been fascinated with the insect world. So the idea of a typewriter that was part insect came together very naturally."

The first Bugwriter to appear in the film is the Clark-Nova, a CIA-like operative who, to Cronenberg's mind, represents a kind of tragic hero. "Clark-Nova is a good guy," Cronenberg asserts, "—or at least as close to a good guy as

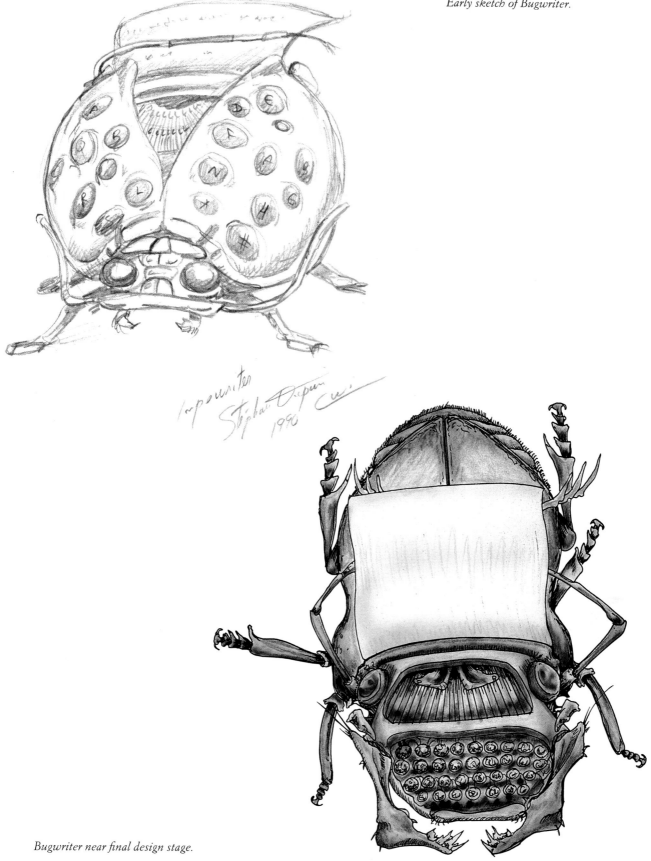

Early sketch of Bugwriter.

Bugwriter near final design stage.

Making the Bugwriter at CWI.

Bugwriter spreads its wings.

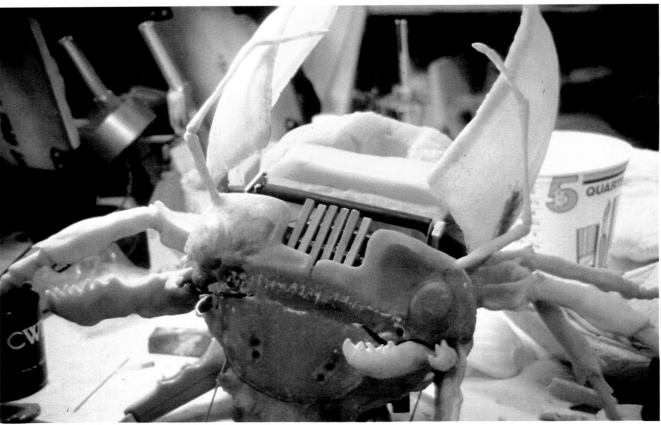

Final prototype at CWI.

you're going to get in Interzone. When he dies in Bill Lee's arms, it is a tragic scene. So Clark-Nova had to have some charm, which made his design somewhat difficult. We went through a lot of design ideas for this guy: How big should he be and how much expression should he have? How much could we rely on real insect anatomy and still get something that would work dramatically? There was a lot of trial and error before we came up with a successful design." Cronenberg and his creature-effects collaborators eventually settled on a Clark-Nova that incorporates both beetle and crablike features, as well as a type-writer keyboard and a sphincter in the back end, from which the creature speaks.

Because of the numerous actions required of the Clark-Nova, thirteen separate puppets had to be constructed. "We had two heros that were used for all the closeup talking scenes,"

Isaac explains. "One was a rod puppet that we used for all the close-ups on the head moving—the jaw, wings, mandibles, and antennas were all capable of movement. That one, which was used for shots of the Clark-Nova scurrying across Lee's desk, also had fully mechanical legs that were operated on a cam con-troller. Then, for the talking sphincter in the back end, we had a second hero Clark-Nova that was a hand puppet. Puppeteer Brian Dewey would put two hands into the back and move his fingers so that he could get a lot of expression out of it as it talked. On that one the front legs moved up and down and side to side, but the back legs were tied down. The head section of that one was also operated by hand—a puppeteer would put his hand inside, holding the jaw and moving it up and down." Additional puppets include a pull-toy rig that was used for shots of the Bugwriter moving across the floor, and a self-contained,

William Burroughs with Bugwriter in the prop room.

motorized "flailer" puppet for shots of the character frantically shaking and waving its appendages.

The most complicated of the Clark-Nova scenes was one in which the beetle typewriter literally consumes the Martinelli. The Martinelli typewriter was conceived as a more streamlined, almost feminine version of the Bugwriter. Cable-controlled, the Martinelli has a more mechanical than organic look, with a keyboard and roller at its top. To facilitate the cannibalism scene, the Martinelli was fitted with breakaway areas—sections of latex foam that were cut out, dressed with hot-pour vinyl to create a stringy, slimy interior, and then lightly stuck back into place. Ultrathin wings were constructed for shots of the Clark-Nova biting and crushing the Martinelli's wings. Demanding the full mechanical capabilities of both the Clark-Nova and the Martinelli, the scene was realized with no fewer than fifteen puppeteers on the set.

In all of the scenes featuring talking mechanical creatures, the puppeteers were aided by the characters' lines being read on the set by an actor hired specifically for that purpose. The most challenging aspect of the *Naked Lunch* project from a creature-effects point of view were the pages and pages of dialogue demanding extensive lip-synching from the mechanical puppets. "We had to find a way to coordinate the lip-synching and the puppeteering and the performances once we got on the set," Isaac notes. "If we had just had our puppeteers read the lines, that could have been distracting to Peter Weller because they are not actors and they would most likely not do justice to the lines. So David auditioned actors and hired one to read all of our characters' lines in the proper rhythm and cadence. Then we taped that so that we could rehearse our puppeteering with

Sex blobs under construction at CWI.

it. On the set, the actor was miked so that our puppeteers below could hear him—and then Peter could hear him live. So Peter had a real voice to play off while the puppet was mouthing the words."

A nontalking though equally challenging effect was required for the transformation of the Arabic typewriter into a quivering, pulsating sex blob. This transformation takes place as Bill Lee and Joan Frost express their lust for each other, typing erotic words on the keyboard of the exotic typewriter. Engineering the scene was complicated by difficulties locating an authentic Arabic typewriter. With time running out, the prop and art departments settled for a sturdy English typewriter that had been heavily used in the field during World War I. "We didn't get the typewriter until very late," Isaac recalls, "so we had to simplify the transformation somewhat. Chris Walas had

already designed the final-stage sex blob, so essentially we had the last stage of something without knowing what the first stage was going to look like."

The transformation begins with the keyboard of the typewriter flipping around, exposing fleshy, breastlike organs. "We had bladders on the top of the typewriter that we could suck in with a suction mechanism and then expand so that the fleshy part would balloon out and begin to pulse. We also had bladders around the entire rim of the typewriter so that it would bulge and begin to change shape. And then, in the back, there was an appendage that grew between the two 'cheeks' of the typewriter," explains Isaac. The second stage of the transformation incorporated additional tentacles topped with typewriter keys. When fully transformed, the sex blob leaps from the desk onto the passionate couple entwined on the floor. As the scene

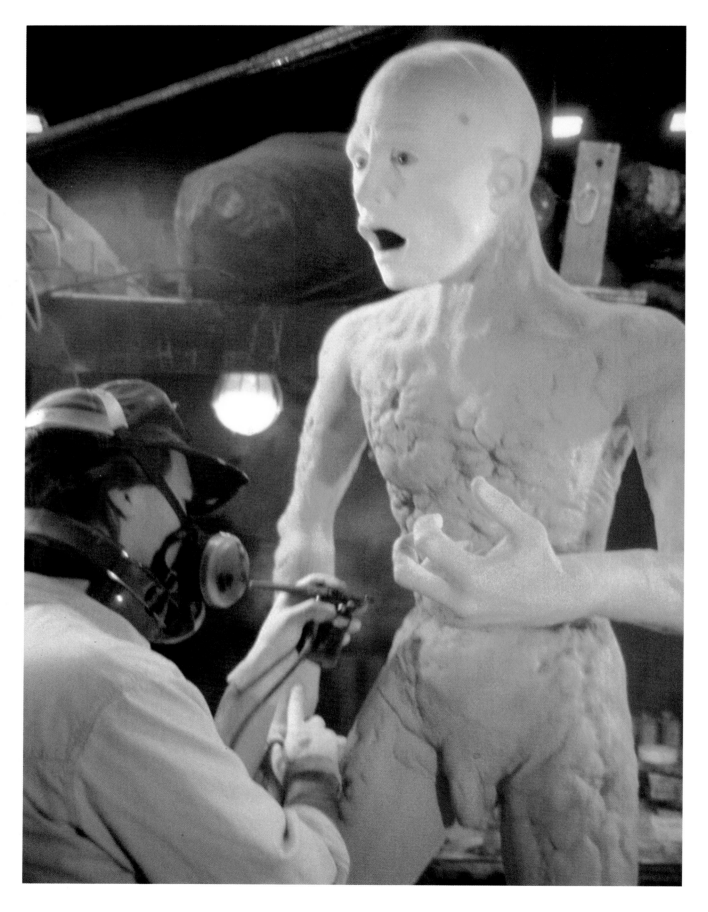

opposite: *Making Kiki at CWI.*

CWI storyboard of Kiki/Cloquet cage scene.

continues, Fadela enters with a whip and beats the out-of-control sex blob until it moves to the balcony, from which it finally jumps. Three sex-blob rigs were constructed to achieve all of the various actions. "We had one that jumped," says Isaac, "and then another one that traveled across the floor as Fadela chased it with the whip. It was self-contained and motorized; we could turn it on by radio control to control its speed. Then we had a third one that was a hand puppet with cam-controlled appendages that flailed around."

Another major mechanical effect was required for the scene in which Yves Cloquet, a wealthy Swiss Anglophile, literally devours the young boy Kiki. In conducting research for *Arachnophobia,* the CWI team had witnessed large spiders eating small mice. Although they found it a gruesome event, the team was also impressed by the graceful finesse with which the

spiders slowly and seductively sucked the juices and removed the skins of their victims. Isaac recalls, "When we described it to David, he really liked the idea of incorporating that same feeling into the scene with Cloquet and Kiki. It is sexual and horrific at the same time."

The scene calls for Cloquet to appear to transform into a centipede as Kiki dissolves. Too complicated to be achieved with makeup, the sequence required full-sized puppet representations of Kiki and Cloquet. "The Cloquet puppet has a centipede body but a face that is still recognizable as the character," says Isaac. "On Kiki's face we had a suction mechanism so that the whole face would sink and disintegrate. Both of the heads were mechanical; the eyes and the necks and jaws moved. The bodies were actually attached together and operated from below with poles. The whole rig was over six feet tall,

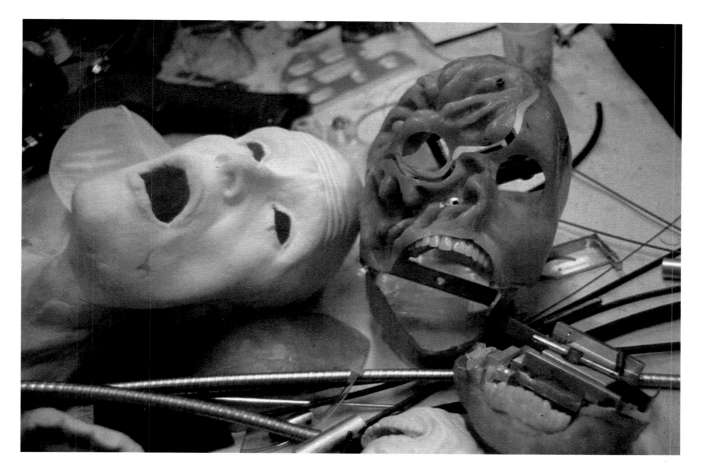

opposite: Cloquet and Kiki model in prop room.

Masks of Kiki and Cloquet at CWI.

so it was a cumbersome thing to operate."

Though the horrific creatures of fantasy were among the film's most demanding effects, CWI was also challenged to create a variety of more straightforward insects, as well as a major makeup gag. CWI's first effect in the film, in fact, is a large talking beetle presented to Lee by two police officers. The six-inch-long "caseworker bug" was realized with five separate beetle rigs, one of which is a fully mechanical version designed, like the Clark-Nova, to talk through a moving sphincter in the back. In addition to the talking beetle, CWI created a variety of centipedes to enhance the insect ambience of particular sequences. In all, forty latex-foam dummy centipedes—ranging from six feet to two feet in length—were constructed.

A major sequence toward the conclusion of the film necessitated elaborate makeup work. As William Lee watches, Fadela transforms to reveal her true identity as Dr. Benway, played by Roy Scheider. This metamorphosis was achieved in two parts. In the first, actress Monique Mercure rips open her chest to reveal the masculine chest of Dr. Benway inside her. Isaac explains, "Monique wore a fiberglass underskull strapped to her body with a foam-rubber chest glued onto it. We had taken a life cast of Roy's chest earlier so that we could make it breathe. Then, over that, we attached a prosthetic piece of *her* chest—the one she rips open. It was split down the middle and connected lightly with KY jelly so that when she grabbed both sides of the skin, it would open easily. With all of these pieces on her—the man's chest and the female chest prosthetic—she was obviously several inches thicker in her torso than she would normally be. But because it was shot from just one angle in the front, that wasn't apparent."

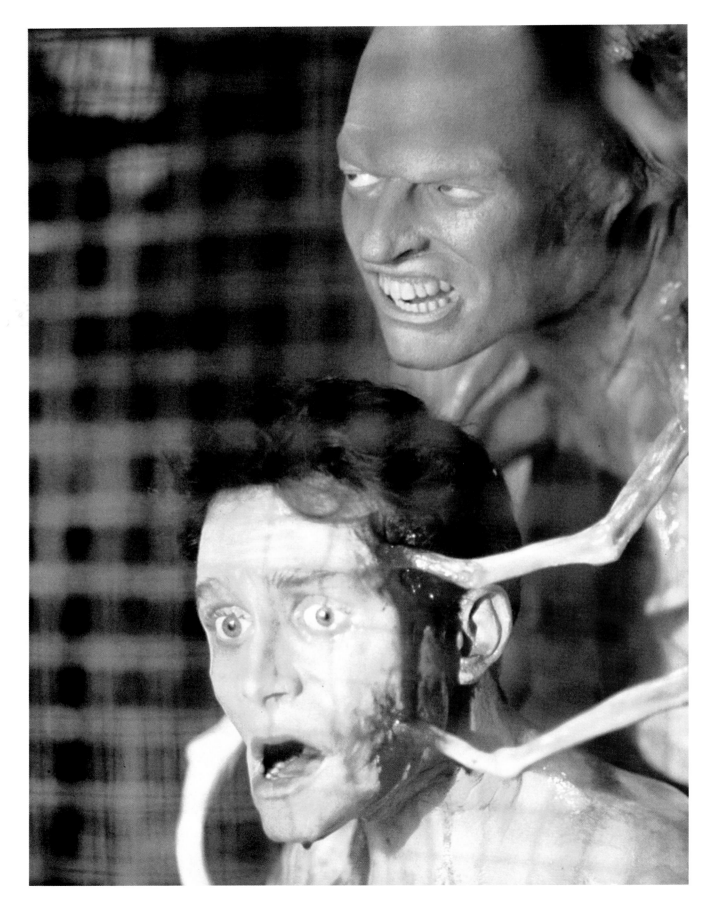

opposite: cage scene of Kiki and Cloquet.

Monique Mercure in Fadela costume.

After Fadela opens her chest up to the neck, the scene cuts to Roy Scheider in a Fadela facial prosthetic. The silicone mold made from a life cast of Monique Mercure was soaked in kerosene to enlarge it by approximately ten percent so that an appropriately sized prosthetic could be made to fit over the larger head of Scheider. Once a facial piece had been made, it was split in two and then reconnected with KY jelly and painted to mask the seam. In the scene, Scheider pulls the skin apart to reveal his own face beneath, and then wears the piece as a kind of cloak throughout the rest of the scene. "The actors were excellent," notes Isaac. "They played both sides of it so well,

they really sold the effect. No matter how well we do our job, it always takes the actor to make that kind of gag believable."

Bringing Cronenberg's bizarre images to the screen occupied the talents of CWI for well over a year. Though the creature and makeup effects for *Naked Lunch* were well conceived and flawlessly executed, their ultimate effectiveness was very much in the hands of the director. "We had every confidence that David would cut the film so that these things weren't too blatant," concludes Jim Isaac. "We knew that he would try to use the effects with some degree of subtlety, leaving something to the audience's imagination."

Jody Duncan is an editor at Cinefex *magazine.*

SO DEEP IN MY HEART
THAT YOU'RE REALLY
A PART OF ME

Chris Rodley

The realization of David Cronenberg's version of William Burroughs's *Naked Lunch* constitutes not only a cinematic inevitability; it is also the latest stage in a filmic experiment that has spanned some twenty years. Like Seth Brundle emerging from the telepod in Cronenberg's film *The Fly,* Peter Weller—as Burroughs's alter ego William Lee—stands before the camera in *Naked Lunch* as the most explicit and successful result to date of that experiment. Brundlefly becomes Burroughs-Cronenberg.

Separation can be a terrifying thing, but so can the reverse. The director has engineered a disintegration and reintegration by embracing the colonizing influence of Burroughs's sensibility in his own life and work. In the process he has been ruthless with the source material; control is the essence of artistic life.

The influence of Burroughs on Cronenberg extends much further than Cronenberg's cinema and operates on several levels. As an aspiring writer Cronenberg was so influenced by the work of Burroughs and Vladimir Nabokov that he felt unable to produce original work as a novelist. For Cronenberg the consumer, Burroughs's work was irresistibly appealing; for Cronenberg the would-be writer, it proved stifling.

From the outset, Burroughs's influence was like a neurological connection. Beyond its startling language and literary form, beyond its "forbidden" subject matter and obsessions (and sympathetic reaction to the repressive era in which it was written), the work spoke most immediately to Cronenberg's viscera. More an infection than an influence.

To coexist with an infection you have to be ingenious or it can subsume all of you. An artistic cure is essential to the creation of work that is intrinsically one's own.

opposite: Jeff Goldblum before his metamorphosis in The Fly.

above: a young Cronenberg on the set of The Parasite Murders, *a.k.a.* Shivers.

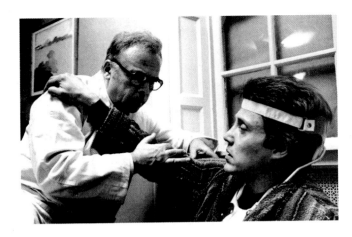

Cronenberg's particular antidote emerged in the act of filmmaking. He felt free to invent his own cinema, to be original in a way he could not with his writing, while many other filmmakers of his generation struggled with cinematic atavism under the towering shadows of Hitchcock, Ford, Hawks, and so on.

Cronenberg is no cinephile. To Cronenberg, what separates Fellini from Paul Brickman, director of *Risky Business,* is the auteurist impulse; the drive to create a discernable, hermetically sealed world consistent from film to film; an instantly recognizable sensibility or vision. There are no direct cinematic influences on Cronenberg's work. His heaviest influences are literary, and Burroughs is perhaps the strongest.

Similarities between the work of Burroughs and Cronenberg arise as much from the sheer force of imagery as from the imagery itself. Finding a cinematic equivalent for a literary vision is one thing; equaling its power in the context of another medium is something else entirely. Cronenberg's compulsion is to "show the unshowable, to speak the unspeakable," and even his relatively subdued and mainstream *Dead Zone* (1983) is filled with images not easily erased from the mind. His ability to imag-ine and create the impossible in ways truly shocking—without compromise, a remarkable feat given the commercial demands informing so much of cinema—is what binds the Cronenbergesque to the Burroughsian. Both artists have suffered from often hysterically adverse reaction to the powerful images they have unleashed, and the impact of their vision has been overshadowed for some audiences by the "disgusting" nature of the subject matter.

It has never been Cronenberg's intention to create an exact translation of Burroughs's writing into film. As he has observed, there exists no possibility of direct translation into filmic language of Burroughs's work. Techniques such as cut-ups, fold-ins, or as in the case of *Naked Lunch,* the montage method are formal strategies that remain unexplored in cinema outside the so-called avant-garde film. The filmic equivalent of Burroughs's manipulation of literary form can be found in the experimental films of Antony Balch, who made several shorts with Burroughs in the early 1960s and who also made extensive plans for his own version of *Naked Lunch* in 1964 but failed to raise the necessary finances.

The Balch-Burroughs collaborations, which prefigured certain elements of the New York underground film movement, were of great interest to a young Cronenberg in the sixties. Despite the appeal that these films (which spoke of sex and drugs and rock and roll) held for Cronenberg living in the repressive state of Ontario, his first two short features, *Stereo* (1969) and *Crimes of the Future* (1970), were not experiments in film as film. The Burroughsian influence in these two remarkably original early films was not reflected in the visuals; nor did they break with conventional form. Rather, it was echoed in the films' voice-overs and the world those voices described. If *Stereo* and

*above: Christopher Walken emerges from
a coma in* The Dead Zone.

Lobby card from
Crimes of the Future.

Lobby card from Stereo.

Crimes of the Future signal the beginning of Cronenberg's own philosophical inquiries in film, they also clearly show where that inquiry has been influenced by, or overlaps with, Burroughs.

Certain elements in these films and Cronenberg's subsequent commercial features seem to be virtually direct references or homages to Burroughs's work. These surface currents of a neurological connection—symptoms, if you will—are iconographic and thematic. Both *Stereo* and *Crimes of the Future* take place in a kind of future that might also be the present and are dominated by tales of control and conspiracy. Control of the mind by drug use, brain surgery, and sophisticated telepathic techniques are central to *Stereo,* as they are to Burroughs's texts.

Conspiracy, another key theme for Burroughs, abounds in *Crimes of the Future* as strange renegade institutions and groups, most notably a heterosexual pedophilic conspiracy, battle to

James Woods in headgear experimenting with "Videodrome" in Videodrome.

The head of the Somafree Institute,
Dr. Raglan (Oliver Reed), is attacked by the Brood.

control an alien situation: most of the female population has fallen victim to a fatal dermatological disease brought on by use of cosmetics. Conspiratorial institutions crop up frequently in Cronenberg's cinema, most explicitly with Consec in *Scanners* (1980) and Spectacular Optical in *Videodrome* (1982). Most of Cronenberg's commercial films feature institutions involved in advanced, covert, or mysterious activities that impact unpredictably on the lives of the protagonists.

Stereo and *Crimes of the Future* introduced the first of Cronenberg's absentee scientists: Dr. Luther Stringfellow (a parapsychologist) and Antione Rouge (a mad dermatologist) respectively, fantastic characters not dissimilar to Burroughs's curious and ambitious Dr. Benway (a forensic psychologist) and Dr. Schafer (a compulsive lobotomizer and experimental surgeon). Cronenberg's roster of doctors includes as well Emil

Lobby card from Rabid.

DUNNING/LINK/REITMAN present **MARILYN CHAMBERS** IN **RABID**

starring JOE SILVER · HOWARD RYSHPAN
and FRANK MOORE as READ
written & directed by DAVID CRONENBERG

James Woods and Deborah Harry in Videodrome.

Hobbes (*Shivers,* 1975), Dan Kelloid (*Rabid,* 1976), Hal Raglan (*The Brood,* 1979), Paul Ruth (*Scanners*), and Professor Brian O'Blivion (*Videodrome*), to name but a few.

Having studied science in college, Cronenberg at one time considered pursuing a career in biochemistry. His interest in scientific endeavors runs deep and is by no means inherited from Burroughs. His various incarnations of scientists as charismatic, eccentric, and at the worst, morally misguided in their sincere efforts to short circuit, aid, or improve the body and the evolutionary process is tinged with more than a little Burroughs. As Schafer says in *Naked Lunch,* "The human body is scandalously inefficient. Instead of a mouth and an anus to get out of order why not have one all-purpose hole to eat and eliminate? We could seal up the nose and mouth, fill in the stomach, make an air hole direct into the lungs where it should have been in the first place. . . ."

The body is the site where Cronenberg and Burroughs overlap most perfectly in concept and image. Both are very body conscious; both are fascinated with the potential of transformation and independent revolution of the flesh; both evince a puritan disgust with the flesh (although at least one of them might deny it); both delve into sex, violence, virus, and disease. And each has focused readily on the threatening or repulsive, rather than the redemptive, aspects of physical revolution, with a very fortunate sense of humor. Burroughs's fascination with mutation, hybrids, regeneration, and to a lesser degree, reincarnation all find a striking visual afterlife in Cronenberg's commercial movies.

Burroughs speaks in *Naked Lunch* of "undifferentiated tissue, which can grow into any kind of flesh . . . sex organs sprout everywhere." In *Crimes of the Future,* at the Institute of Neo-Venereal Disease, Adrian Tripod (Ron Mlodzik) meets a friend

who is indeed growing mysterious, functionless organs. And in *Rabid* Rose (Marilyn Chambers) develops a penislike syringe in her armpit as the result of a radical plastic surgery technique that treats patients with morphogenetically neutral skin grafts. Disciples of "Psychoplasmics" in *The Brood* develop all manner of fleshy manifestations; most notably Nola Carveth (Samantha Eggar) creates little monster children complete with cleft palettes, air sacks, and direct telepathic connection with the "mother ship." In *Videodrome* Max Renn (James Woods) hallucinates an abdominal vagina, a hand-gun and grenade, and flesh-ripping death by internal cancer explosions.

Burroughs first came across the name of Cronenberg on the release of *Scanners*. He found the idea of the exploding head sequence intriguing. The movie returns to the primary theme of *Stereo*: telepathy. Much of Burroughs's work revolves around the power of the mind to control the flesh of others and to affect the physical world in dramatic ways, and around the power of writing. The political side of *Scanners* too finds a parallel in *Naked Lunch*. Just as Cronenberg's telepathic mutants are appropriated by intelligence organizations or oppositional terrorist groups as Darryl Revok and his disciples aim to control the planet, in *Naked Lunch* Burroughs's Senders have apparently gained this ability. With *Dead Ringers* (1988) the conjoined interests of Cronenberg and Burroughs reaches its ultimate as the movie unfolds the story of identical twin gynecologists Elliot and Beverly Mantle: two bodies, two minds, one soul.

In Cronenberg's remake of *The Fly* (1986), Seth Brundle (Jeff Goldblum) slowly mutates into a new life after having been accidentally fused at the molecular level with a housefly. Although Burroughs usually uses insect metaphor to describe the soulless or inhuman and, by contrast, Cronenberg finds a strange beauty in insect life (hence the sympathy elicited for Brundlefly), the interface between human and insect is remarkably similar for Cronenberg and Burroughs. Cronenberg's original working title for *Rabid,* a modern vampire story in which Rose finds herself able to digest nothing but blood, which she sucks up through her newly acquired penile appendage, was *Mosquito.* Characters transform into giant centipedes in *Naked Lunch.* Perhaps Brundlefly said it best in *The Fly:* "I'm saying I'm an insect who dreamt he was a man and loved it. But now the dream is over and the insect is awake."

Burroughs and Cronenberg share the view that disease is

Jeremy Irons plays twin doctors in Dead Ringers.

opposite: exploding head sequence from Scanners.

an intelligent life form, not merely something that must be destroyed before it destroys. Burroughs sees it as a basic part of life ("what came first, the intestine or the tapeworm?") that takes many uncommon forms. In Cronenberg's *Shivers,* Nurse Forsythe (Lynn Lowry) relates a dream in which she has been told that "disease is the love of two kinds of alien creatures for each other." A notice in the surgeon's waiting room reads SEX IS THE INVENTION OF A CLEVER VENEREAL DISEASE. And the fecal-phallic parasites in *Shivers* bear a strong resemblance to Burroughs's lecherous candiru in *Naked Lunch:* "small eel-like fish or worm . . . long patronizing certain rivers of ill repute."

Seth Brundle asserts in *The Fly* that contagion isn't the problem because he "knows what the disease wants." What it wants is to turn him into something else, something that never existed before. Cronenberg's interest, like Burroughs's, is not

Jeff Goldblum and Cronenberg on the set of The Fly.

117

only in the disease's point of view (*Shivers* earned Cronenberg the accolade "King of Venereal Horror"), but in its function as an agent of change, as a factor in the evolutionary process. In Burroughs's story "The Astronaut's Return," an ancient parasite—"what Freud calls the unconscious"—is spawned in the caves of Europe on human flesh irradiated in a nuclear explosion some thirty thousand years ago. Declaring that "the descendants of [these] cave-dwelling albinos are the present inhabitants of America and Western Europe," Burroughs credits a virus with the entirety of historical, political, cultural, and evolutionary processes.

To some extent, explicitly Burroughsian imagery has gradually been exorcised from Cronenberg's work. Critic Mitch Tuchman asserted in 1984 that "without Burroughs, Cronenberg may be without imagery." Despite this harsh assessment, Cronenberg by then had already entered a new phase in his development as a director: a more interior, melancholic, and mature period, less concerned with special effects and altogether divorced from his "schlock-horror" past. Cronenberg continues to pursue an increasingly personal vision, as is abundantly clear in his version of *Naked Lunch*.

Although both were raised in middle-class North America, Burroughs and Cronenberg couldn't be more different. And while they share numerous common interests, there remain great differences in their work. None of Burroughs's impassioned moralism and belief in an afterlife appears in Cronenberg's work. In the Cronenberg universe there are no external forces; man alone creates and re-creates the world. Nuclear holocaust, should it happen, is our natural end. And yet the vital neurological connection between Burroughs and Cronenberg has resulted in some of the most unique cinema to have emerged since the seventies.

In 1981 Cronenberg told *Omni* magazine, "Some part of me would love to make a movie of William Burroughs's *Naked Lunch*." As one critic observed three years later, some part of him already had.

Chris Rodley is a filmmaker and documentarian.

FILMOGRAPHY

Feature films by
David Cronenberg

Stereo, 1969

Crimes of the Future, 1970

The Parasite Murders (also known as *Shivers*
and *They Came from Within*), 1975

Rabid, 1976

Fast Company, 1979

The Brood, 1979

Scanners, 1980

Videodrome, 1982

The Dead Zone, 1983

The Fly, 1986

Dead Ringers, 1988

Naked Lunch, 1992

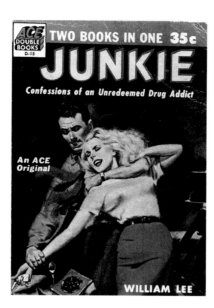

Gary Indiana
·

urroughs's work tends to affect people like a Rorschach test. It separates cultural conservatives from avant-gardists, social reactionaries from libertarians. Or, to use one of Burroughs's favorite distinctions, members of the Johnson Family from the Shits. Johnsons have a live-and-let-live, mind-their-own-business mentality. Shits have an uncontrollable need to pass judgment on and be RIGHT about everything. In today's censorious climate, police work dominates the pages of the book reviews: this writer has the wrong attitude and must be done away with.

Burroughs has always elicited a testy response from the cultural establishment. While early support for *Naked Lunch* from such mandarins as Mary McCarthy and John Ciardi has been matched over the years by encomiums from many of our best writers and by a substantial body of excellent academic criticism, the overall literary world's recognition of Burroughs has been grudging more often than not. Perhaps Burroughs's achievement represents a threat to the well-mannered, conventionally crafted, middle-class novel. It could be as simple as that. Burroughs expanded the content of fiction, giving artistic form to extremes of contemporary abjection. *Naked Lunch* opened a path into the world of the addict, the homosexual, the social outlaw. From this despised and largely unmentionable territory Burroughs extracted a presiding metaphor of Control. *Naked Lunch* deals with the control of consciousness and behavior through addiction—to sex, power, money, drugs, even to control itself. When themes of this nature, which ultimately have to do with politics, lie at the heart of a writer's work, appreciation is often checked by the timidity of those who prefer not to think about such issues.

opposite: William Burroughs, photograph © 1974 Gerard Malanga.

above: cover of Junkie *by "William Lee."*

Burroughs also revolutionized the structure of fiction. He opened the novel to chance operations, using the "cut-up" and "fold-in" techniques he had developed with Brion Gysin and Ian Sommerville. Earlier writers like Conrad sometimes bring the same characters from one novel to the next. Burroughs recycles phrases, "routines," descriptions, and characters through successive works as if they were musical figures or colors in a paint box. His novels suggest an artful arrangement of blocks of prose rather than linear compositions. *Naked Lunch* and the successive books mined from the thousand-some pages Burroughs produced while in and out of heroin addiction in the 1950s—*Nova Express, The Soft Machine, The Ticket That Exploded* (and, recently exhumed, *Interzone*)—compose, in advance of postmodern theory, the first truly postmodern literary texts. Eliminating classical armature and syntax, these books embrace the fragmentary, the "incomplete," the deconstructive.

No doubt the unconventional approach taken by this work inspires nightmares of literary anarchy—what if everyone started writing this way or started writing about what Burroughs writes about? This two-pronged assault on traditional fiction came as the third and arguably furthest-sweeping wave of the Beat movement after Ginsberg's *Howl* and Kerouac's *On the Road.* These set a generation in motion and helped spawn the '60s counterculture. Burroughs deserves consideration apart from the Beats, but there is no doubt that *Naked Lunch* seemed,

on publication, the literary apotheosis of that movement. One obvious difference between *Naked Lunch* and Beat literature is what Mary McCarthy called Burroughs's aerial perspective. Long exiled from the United States—in Mexico, Peru, France, and Morocco—Burroughs takes a long, jaundiced, global view of things. His evocation of America, though suffused with a gelid sort of nostalgia for the sexual dawn of adolescence, lacks entirely the provincial romanticism found in much Beat writing. (Problematically, much of Burroughs's work does share the Beats' extreme gynophobia; one can only defend his remarks about women in *The Job* by noting the misanthropy in his writing overall.)

In any event, Burroughs's absence from the United States during much of the Beat era and the subsequent hippie movement encourages us to link him with British Pop Art as well as The Velvet Underground, with Godard's Alpha 60 as well as *Wild in the Streets.* At this distance, it's tricky to separate quintessentially "Burroughsian" ideas from ideas that were generally in the wind in the '60s. Widespread disgust with and revolt against the gray Cold War conformity of the 1950s was certainly fueled by the Beats and a constellation of associated writers and artists. Strategies of transcendence and escape flowed from such disparate sources as Marxist theory and LSD. Linguistics, along with comparative anthropology, became a countercultural preoccupation. Nonverbal communication loomed as a great undiscovered continent; the nature of the prelinguistic brain was much speculated about. These crypto-

scientific interests of the radical young, which existed alongside a vogue for Eastern mysticism and magical operations, coincided with Burroughs's artistic and personal quest for a "breakthrough in the gray room." A radical interrogation of language permeates his books. As we can see from variously reproduced pages from Burroughs's scrapbooks, his word-and-image experiments closely parallel certain contemporaneous artifacts like Eduoardo Paolozzi's silkscreen series *Moonstrips Empire News* (itself inspired by Wittgenstein's *Philosophical Investigations*), and slightly later work by Joseph Kosuth. (Burroughs has collaborated, both visually and verbally, with Robert Rauschenberg, David Hockney, George Condo, Philip Taaffe, and Keith Haring; in recent years he's been enjoying a second career as a painter.)

Burroughs has always written for the Space Age. His work addresses readers who want OUT of present slave-planet conditions. His theory of language as a virus is closely connected to an (ambivalent) repudiation of Western consciousness in favor of "the savage mind." (This theme, a favorite of '60s culture, is deftly conveyed in Barbet Schroeder's film *The Valley Obscured by Clouds*.) In the tense-scrambled, oneiric narratives of *Nova Express* and *The Ticket That Exploded*, Burroughs invokes the synchronic, telepathic mind of the aboriginal, linking the hieroglyphic "Mayan control calendar" with the image manipulation of contemporary mass media. Other texts, exploring the mind-altering possibilities of Korzybski's general semantics and the Scientology E-meter, read like manuals for dismantling prerecorded consciousness. Burroughs's basic project is psychoanalytic: to discard imprints, received ideas, the residue of psychic wounds, all forms of false consciousness. Since he pictures liberation as a state of tranquility and "mineral silence" rather than one of religious or sexual ecstasy, this goal seems close to Freud's ambition to replace neurotic unhappiness with ordinary unhappiness.

Being a novelist instead of a theoretician, Burroughs invariably paints the catastrophic possibilities inherent in any scheme of liberation. His pointed refusal to endorse "the garden

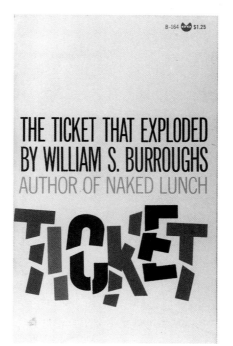

of delights" of the psychedelic movement, though widely ignored at the time, reflects the stubborn complexity of a born realist. A strain of solid common sense serves as a bracket around writing uncommonly open to the apocalyptic imagination. It's difficult to pinpoint the precise amount of put-on in the dozens of texts Burroughs contributed, in the '60s and '70s, to English and American underground newspapers, describing methods for instigating riots and disrupting the urban infrastructure. The chill-blooded revolutionary stance is seldom struck without irony; prescriptions for poisoning water supplies or launching biological warfare often turn up later as "routines" in Burroughs's fictions like *The Wild Boys* and *Blade Runner: A Movie.* Nevertheless, it's worth remembering that between roughly 1967 and 1973, the mood of much of the West was apocalyptic; authentic populist movements really did threaten the control mechanisms of the media-military-industrial complex, for the first and only time since World War II. Burroughs's writings were part of a seminal, restive cultural mix that included Herbert Marcuse, N. O. Brown, Frantz Fanon, Claude Levi-Strauss, and Marshall McLuhan—which in turn influenced musicians such as John Cage and LaMonte Young; diverse artists including R. J. Kitaj, Robert Rauschenberg, Yoko Ono, and Jasper Johns; numerous theater directors such as Jean-Claude van Italie, Joseph Chaikin, and Julian Beck; innumerable writers; and filmmakers Nicholas Roeg, Vera Chytilova, Alessandro Jodorowski, the Godard of *One Plus One* and *Weekend,* and the Pasolini of *Pigpen,* to name only a few.

Burroughs has remained an influential figure throughout the last two decades, partly on the strength of later novels like *Exterminator!, Port of Saints, Cities of the Red Night, The Place of Dead Roads,* and *The Western Lands,* in which earlier experimental procedures have been integrated into more traditionally coherent narratives. Another part of Burroughs's appeal, especially to younger readers, is the prophetic aura of his books. *Naked Lunch,* for example, refers ahead twenty years to liposuction ("stomach tucks"), autoerotic asphyxia, and a fatal AIDS-like viral epidemic. Some of his writing is uncanny in this respect. Some of it simply identifies problems that recur and magnify themselves historically: for example, drug hysteria, a relatively minor tool of social repression in the 1940s and 1950s, today a major implement of state terror. The "purple-assed baboon" routine, used in "Roosevelt After Inauguration" to satirize Roosevelt's attempt to pack the Supreme Court, also anticipates the neoconservative take-over of the American judiciary in the 1980s and 1990s.

The culture has absorbed many of Burroughs's ideas so thoroughly that their source is now obscured. A conspiratorial view of government didn't originate with Burroughs, but he was the first American novelist to make justified paranoia a major literary theme. The idea of sinister forces controlling the world of appearances is commonplace in post-Watergate, post–Iran Contra America, but it was considered bizarre and unseemly when Burroughs invented the Nova Mob.

The pitch-black humor and rejection of humanism in Burroughs's works were naturally embraced by the punk movement, notably by Patti Smith. In the distinctly unpsychedelic and junk-ridden milieu of downtown Manhattan in the late '70s, Burroughs was elder statesman, guru, and cautionary presence all in one. It would be foolish to claim that the strong antijunk message of *Naked Lunch* ever dissuaded a single junkie, or indeed was ever intended to. Both the courtroom transcripts from the 1966 Boston obscenity trial and Burroughs's "Deposition: Testimony Concerning a Sickness" that preface all later editions of *Naked Lunch* serve exactly the same satirical purpose as the frontispiece disclaimers and pledges of high moral altitude that accompany any picaresque novel out to shock, from Defoe's *Roxana* to Nabokov's *Lolita.* In the '70s *Naked Lunch* was to junkies what *Alice in Wonderland* and *The Hobbit* were to acidheads in the '60s. In other words, a completely accurate guide to what you could expect if you got addicted to heroin. In the days before AIDS, many people wanted, for reasons of their own, to go through hell and (maybe) live to tell about it. Burroughs's writings were useful in the sense that reading them kept you from being too deluded about what you were doing.

The extravagant homoeroticism of *The Wild Boys* and *Cities of the Red Night* echoes in the films of Derek Jarman, which also employ the aleatory cutting techniques of Burroughs's fiction. The device of anachronism in *Cities of the Red Night*—a formally tidy variant of the "time travel" produced by scrambled texts in earlier works—crops up in Jarman's *Caravaggio,* Rudy Wurlitzer and Alex Cox's film *Walker,* and a recent novel by William Gibson and Bruce Sterling, *The Difference Engine.* Burroughs's literary influence on Kathy Acker, Dennis Cooper, David Wojnarowicz, and myself is as various as we are and probably something for others to elucidate.

Repetitive variations of the cut-up method using tape recorders and film, investigated by Burroughs in collaboration with Ian Sommerville and Antony Balch, have been adapted in music by Philip Glass, Gavin Bryers (the looping in *The Sinking of the Titanic,* in particular), and Glenn Branca (*Symphony #2*), among others; groups like The Insect Trust, Steely Dan, Hüsker Dü, and Throbbing Gristle have named themselves out of *Naked Lunch* and/or applied Burroughs's techniques of composition. Burroughs has made numerous recordings combining readings of his work with experimental music, including the highly successful *Dead City Radio,* as well as other recordings made in collaboration with Giorno Poetry Systems. He recently collaborated with Robert Wilson and Tom Waits on *The Black Rider,* a music drama. Though imperfectly realized, the picture book projects *Ah Pook Is Here* and *The Book of Breeething* were sufficiently well known to have informed the recent outgrowth of "graphic novels"—grown-up comic books by serious writers such as Clive Barker and Michael Moorcock, intended to catch

NOVA EXPRESS
WILLIAM S. BURROUGHS
A NOVEL BY THE AUTHOR OF NAKED LUNCH

the short, primarily visual attention span of the TV-and-Nintendo generation.

The question of how Burroughs's themes, characters, and ideas might be communicated to a wider audience remains complicated in 1991. Because certain important aspects of the work—explicit homoerotica and homoerotic violence, defecatory fantasies, etc.—are not only controversial but banned from mainstream film and from television, Burroughs's mythology for the Space Age has "entered the mainstream" at an oblique angle. Religious hysteria surrounding the depiction of sexuality and bodily functions is a depressing, near-universal fact of life today. However, it would be insultingly reductive to suggest that Burroughs's achievement consists entirely in his exemplary frankness about sucking and fucking. His invention of alternative worlds, of creatures like the Mugwumps, the Green Boys, and the Nova Mob, and archetypal characters like Bradley the Buyer, A. J. the After-Birth Tycoon, Hamburger Mary, and Dr. Benway represents a protean effort of imagination. Some of Burroughs's complex insights into the social dynamics of addiction—and a good deal of Burroughsian humor—were incorporated into Gus Van Sant's *Drugstore Cowboy,* a film that features Burroughs as a defrocked junkie priest. Though Ridley Scott adopted the title rather than the story of Burroughs's *Blade Runner,* the movie's cast of renegade androids and its bosky, evocative ambiance—Piranesian architectural and human ruins outscaled by the monolithic "Mayan pyramids" of the corporate future—belong to Burroughs's fictional world, as does the device of Scott's *Alien,* i.e., a parasite that eventually consumes and assimilates its host organism. Among major filmmakers, it's undoubtedly David Cronenberg, now director of the movie *Naked Lunch,* whose imagination most closely parallels Burroughs's own. The lethal telepathic practices of *Scanners,* TV-induced brain tumors and "organic" video cassettes in *Videodrome,* fatal symbiosis between twins in *Dead Ringers,* and even—especially—the disembodied gall bladder that swims up between Barbara Steele's legs in *The Parasite Murders* correspond to the queasily visceral marriages of flesh and technology pioneered by *Naked Lunch, The Soft Machine,* and *Nova Express.* More pertinent still is the crisply detached "paranoid realism" practiced by both artists: the sense that every human interaction contains the possibility of homicide. Or, as the title of Alan Ansen's 1959 essay on Burroughs put it, "Anyone Who Can Pick Up a Frying Pan Owns Death."

Gary Indiana is a novelist, playwright, and culture critic.

FICTION

by
William S. Burroughs

Photography and Illustration Credits

All photographs except those noted below are by Brian Hamill and Attila Dory, © 1992 Naked Lunch Productions, Ltd. and Recorded Picture Company, Ltd.

page 12 © 1984 Kate Simon

page 14 courtesy of Don Kennison

pages 66, 68, 70 drawings by Carol Spier © 1992 Naked Lunch Productions, Ltd. and Recorded Picture Company, Ltd.

pages 90, 95, 96, 99, 105 drawings © 1992 Chris Walas, Inc.

pages 91–92, 94, 97–98, 100–104, 107 © 1992 Chris Walas, Inc.

pages 110–15, 117 courtesy of Cinematheque, Toronto, Ontario

page 116 courtesy of David Cronenberg

page 120 © 1974 Gerard Malanga, courtesy of Grove Press

page 121, 122 bottom courtesy of Rob Warren

pages 120 top, 121–22 courtesy of Ira Silverberg